TVB
E3

Kirkby Stephen

Also available from Kirkby Stephen Press:
The History and Traditions of Mallerstang Forest and Pendragon Castle
by Rev. W. Nicholls
ISBN 978-0-9928045-0-3

Kirkby Stephen

Essays on the history of town and landscape

With a selection of drawings from the
nineteenth century sketchbook of
Thomas Fawcett of Kirkby Stephen

Peter McWilliam BA (Hons), MA (Hons)

Kirkby Stephen Press

Kirkby Stephen Press
Birkbeck Gardens, Kirkby Stephen, Cumbria CA17 4TH

ISBN 978-0-9928045-1-0

Printed by H. Charlesworth & Co Ltd., Wakefield
Typeset by Pinnacle Graphic Design Ltd., Ilkley, West Yorkshire

Illustrations on verso chapter title pages by Jane Tilley -
spiderweb@spiderweb.plus.com
Buck's drawings of Brough, Hartley and Pendragon Castles courtesy Mark Peatfield
Other location maps based on the Ordnance Survey 1:25000 First Series NY70/80
Contents of T. Fawcett's Sketchbook in Chapter Seven: Cumbria Archive Service,
Kendal. WDX1137/1

To Jenny

Contents

List of Maps & Illustrations

Introduction   1

1. Early Settlement   9

2. The Anglo-Scottish Border   29

3. The Pilgrimage of Grace, 1536/7   45

4. The Wharton's of Wharton Hall, Kirkby Stephen   59

5. The Wharton & Ravenstonedale Deer Parks   77

6. Kirkby Stephen Town & River: Mills & Manufacture   87

7. Thomas Fawcett's Sketchbook   119

8. Upper Eden Upland: Introduction   141

9. Upper Eden Upland: Hartley Fell & Nine Standards   147

10. Upper Eden Upland: Mallerstang   161

11. Upper Eden Upland: Wild Boar Fell & The Clouds   179

    Further Reading   193

List of Maps & Illustrations

(The Transactions of the Cumberland & Westmorland Antiquarian & Archaeological Society Series One, Two & Three have been abbreviated to CW1, 2 or 3 in references).

	Page
1. An outline map of Kirkby Stephen & Upper Eden today	3
2. Kirkby Stephen & district Parish & Township maps	7
3. The Crosby Garrett helmet	12
4. Crosby Garrett helmet find location site	13
5. Routes through Mallerstang	15
6. The badly eroded stump of Rey Cross, Stainmore	18
7. The Upper Eden valley in Roman times	18
8. Sketch map of the Roman road at Brough	20
9. Buck's drawing of the south-east view of Brough Castle	24
10. The modern ruin of Brough Castle	25
11. Drove roads of Westmorland	27
12. The Anglo-Scottish Border	32
13. Two views of Silver Street	33
14. High walls and narrow passageways - Faraday Road and Little Wiend	34
15. Croft Street, Kirkby Stephen	35
16. Kirkby Stephen town from the first edition six inch to one mile OS map.	37
17. The Loki Stone	38
18. Carlisle in the reign of Elizabeth 1	41
19. Map of the Pilgrimage of Grace	48
20. The ruin of Lammerside Castle	49
21. An effigy of Thomas, first Lord Wharton	51
22. Map of Baronial Halls and Castles in the Upper Eden Valley	53
23. The Wharton pedigree	62
24. The Parish Church of St. Stephen, Kirkby Stephen	65
25. Plan of Wharton Hall near Kirkby Stephen	66
26. An original drawing of Wharton Hall, Westmorland	71
27. The upper reaches of Swaledale	73
28. The remains of the Blakethwaite mines, Gunnerside Gill.	75
29. The northern perimeter of Ravenstonedale Park deer wall	80
30. Outline map of the Wharton Park deer wall	82
31. Outline map of the Ravenstonedale Park deer wall	84
32. A photograph of the Wharton deer wall with original topstones	85
33. 'The Stocking Market, Kirkby Stephen. 1817' by Thomas Fawcett.	93
34. Old Shambles, Market Street, Kirkby Stephen	94
35. Location map for New Bridge, Kirkby Stephen	97
36. Map of road layout before New Bridge	97
37. Map of Kirkby Stephen water mills	97
38. Map of Kirkby Stephen Low mills in the nineteenth century	98
39.1. Low Mill weir from an old postcard	99
39.2. Dam and sluice above the former Low Mill	99

List of Maps & Illustrations cont.

39.3 Low Mill race on Hartley road from an old postcard 99
40. Photograph of ruined smithy at Outhgill, Mallerstang 101
41.1 Frank's Bridge, from a postcard c. 1920 103
41.2 Sketch map of Kirkby Stephen Mill and weir 103
42. Map of Frank's Bridge and surrounding area 104
43. Former Union Cotton Mill and later workhouse, Kirkby Stephen 105
44. Section of Hartley Tithe map, 1839 illustrating the position of Hartley High Mill 106
45. Demolished corn mill at Ravenstonedale from a photograph 107
46. Section of Kirkby Stephen Tithe map with Stenkrith Mill 108
47. Stenkrith Mill based on a drawing by Thomas Fawcett 109

Images of Stenkrith
48. Photograph of Stenkrith Bridge 110
49. Close up photograph of Stenkrith Bridge 110
50. Photograph of demolished hydro-electric station at Stenkrith Bridge 111
51. Photograph of remains of a banked mill race at Stenkrith Park. 111

Drawings from the Fawcett Sketchbook:
52. William Coats' house on what is now North Road called Sparrow Hall 122
53. Between the Parish Church and Low Mill an area called The Green etc 123
54. Bull baiting on Market Square 124
55. The east side of upper Market Street 125
56. Continuing on upper Market Street.... 126
57. The west side of upper Market Street or Fletcher Hill 127
58. On the west side of Market Street 129
59. The Crown Inn and The Red Lion on Market Street 131
60. The Red Lion and Croft House on Market Street 132
61. Facing the Square on Market Street 133
62. The Shambles, Market Street 134
63/4. Mr Powley's Assembly Rooms on upper Market Street 135
65. Townhead House on High Street 137
66. Group of thatch't houses on Primrose Hill 138
67. Blacklins Old Corn and Saw Mill on Riverside 139
68. A view of Sower Pow 140

69. Outline map of Upper Eden upland 144
70. The east view of Harcla Castle (Buck) 149
71. Enlarged view of lower section of Buck's engraving 149
72. Map of Hartley Birkett and Hartley Fell 150
73. Hartley Birkett from the 1st edition six inch to one mile OS map 152
74. Photograph of Lord's Stone 153
75. The Nine Standards on Hartley Fell 154
76. Map of Nine Standards and Tailbridge with mine and quarry sites 154
77. A section of Hodgson's map of Westmorland (1829) 156
78. The Grey Stone (BS) on the old Swaledale - Mallerstang boundary 157

List of Maps & Illustrations cont.

79. Looking north into Dukerdale   159
80. Old coal excavations on Tailbridge Hill above the B6270   159
81. Map of The Scars of Mallerstang Edge   164
82. Looking north to Hangingstone Scar, Mallerstang Edge   165
83. Looking north to Mallerstang Edge from The Highway   166
84. The 'lonely field' at Greenlaw on the lower northerly slopes of Wild Boar Fell   168
85. The North West view of Pendragon Castle (Buck)   168
86. Map of Great Bell, Bleakham, High Pike and Fells End Quarry   169
87. Great Bell and Long Crag with extensive hushing   170
88. Pendragon Castle today   171
89.1 Stone shelter north of Fells End Quarry   172
89.2 Ruined buildings at Fells End Quarry   172
90. Map of Lindrigg and Coalwell Scars   173
91. Stone Close on Mallerstang Common   174
92. A bield on the fellside   175
93. The ruins of Mallerstang Colliery   175
94. Lady's Pillar   176
95. Map of South Mallerstang   177
96. Raven's Nest, Mallerstang   178
97. Millstone cut out above Sand Tarn   182
98. Sand Tarn   182
99. Map of Wild Boar Fell   183
100. Looking south to Wild Boar Fell from Little Fell   184
101. Map of Clouds, Ravenstonedale   188

Images of Clouds, Ravenstonedale
102.1 Looking north to Fell End Clouds   189
102.2 A solitary tree   189
102.3 An old enclosure with fell ponies   190
102.4 Looking north from Dale Slack   190
103. Detail of Clouds from the 1st edition six inch to one mile OS map.   191

Introduction

The Cloisters from a postcard c. 1920

An outline of Kirkby Stephen & Upper Eden today

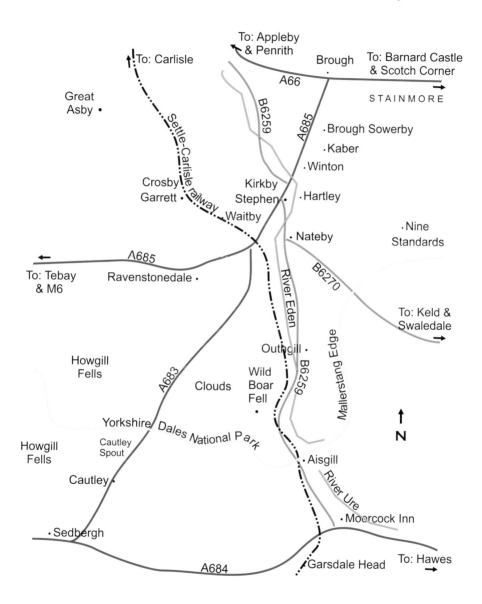

A little of what follows in these chapters was published locally in the new millennium and is now out of print. The content has been substantially reworked to provide a more coherent narrative. It follows the author's interest in both the town and landscape that encircles Kirkby Stephen - the Upper Eden upland - and how this landscape has evolved and been exploited through time. In addition some of its political history has been a microcosm of important developments at regional and national levels.

This volume is best described as a meander through some of the pages of Kirkby Stephen town history and its encircling upland landscape although it does not claim to be either comprehensive or inclusive of its many branches. The aim has been to select subjects where in some cases local matters interfaced with broader historical themes; the Roman interlude, the Anglo- Scottish Border, the Pilgrimage of Grace and the fortunes of one dynastic family - the Whartons of Wharton Hall. In more recent times consideration is also given, for example, to small scale mineral extraction (particularly lead) and how the Wharton family came to seize the regional initiative in Swaledale by developing lead mining on an industrial scale. It was the fourth Lord Wharton who was responsible for developing this mining enterprise. The fifth Lord ('Honest Tom') gained national significance with the formation of the Whig party* and was closely involved in overthrowing the reforming monarchy of James II in 1688 with the 'Glorious Revolution'. Although by this time the family had long since ceased to reside at Wharton Hall. James II had endeavoured to introduce religious toleration to encourage mercantile growth and civil liberty. The fifth Lord was instrumental in this process and made the invitation to William of Orange to take the English throne. As already stated this volume makes no claim to be original but rather is an attempt to create a coherent narrative from the perspective of the locality of Kirkby Stephen. As such *Kirkby Stephen* is intended as a guide for the general reader without the encumbrance of detailed references. One exception is Chapter 6 where, because of the difficulty of providing a detailed historical narrative, references have been supplied to ensure that the evidence that is available is seen to be as secure as possible. It may also encourage other researchers to develop some of the themes explored in this chapter in relation to, by way of example, textile activity for which little evidence now remains.

Kirkby Stephen and its hinterland forms part of what could be called a marginal region of North Pennine upland. Other marginal regions would include wetlands, heathlands and perhaps even a Roman margin. But these marginals have a proper place in the natural order of things. Upper Eden has a distinctive 'feel' and culture but also remains fully integrated within the national economy. In France the word *pays* refers to an area whose inhabitants share a common identity and where cultural, economic and social interests coincide. In a way Kirkby Stephen and the Upper Eden valley displays this kind of identity and continues to offer fascinating glimpses of

---

*Between 1680 and 1850 the Whigs emerged from being a faction to a parliamentary political party contesting power with their rivals, the Tories. Whigs were originally opposed to the absolute rule of the Stuart kings and Roman Catholicism. The "Whig Supremacy" of full government control lasted from 1715 - 1760 following the Hanoverian succession of George 1. At this stage both Whig and Tory parties were managed by wealthy politicians and when only a small number of individuals controlled voters. Whigs supported religious toleration (non conforming Protestants) whilst nearly all Tories supported the established Church of England. Later Whigs supported industrial interests and free trade and Tories the landed interest.

a shared, common past based for ordinary people, as elsewhere, on little more than survival.

This is apparent in some antiquarian accounts such as *The History and Traditions of Mallerstang Forest* first published in 1883 which describes the centuries old communal life of this remote dale just south of Kirkby Stephen. Written by a dissenting clergyman, Rev. William Nicholls, the book portrays a medieval culture of deference and hierarchy whilst acknowledging that the world in his time was changing as a result of modern, democratic forces. *Feudalism rendered its service in its day,* (Nicholls wrote) *but that day has gone, and all the influences of our age are working in an opposite direction.* Not least, in Kirkby Stephen, with the coming of the railway. Nicholls notes *the rude habits of the people. They were not civilised, as we recognise the meaning of that word; they were in the main, however, honest and truthful, and vigorous. They were self-reliant, and shrewd in their business relations with a sharp eye to the main chance.* The old world, *of bygone days, when the dale was more self-contained...and the people realised themselves more fully to be a community of themselves, rather than as a fringe of a great population.*

The inclusion of a social document such as The Fawcett Sketchbook serves to illustrate in graphic and sometimes humorous terms what conditions were like in Kirkby Stephen in the nineteenth century. In earlier times life was difficult and historians now have a sense of the complexity of, for example, the medieval economy and both how inventive and commercial people were and continued to be. Examples here could include the itinerant droving way of life that skirted the Eden valley and more particularly T.S. Willan's *An Eighteenth Century Shopkeeper, Abraham Dent of Kirkby Stephen* which documents the business records of this shopkeeper from the 1750's to the 1780's. Dent had a diverse range of business activities which included stationery, grocery, sundries and then branched into hosiery, wine and brewing. Some of his ventures were not a success and probably his diverse activities were not typical. Since only Dent's business records had survived many questions remain about the broader context of his activities. But other accounts of inland trading do indicate that a considerable network of commercial activity was in place across the country and reached such remote places as Kirkby Stephen as Daniel Defoe discovered on his tour.

To generalise about Kirkby Stephen's place within the regional network of what is now Cumbria, the former county of Westmorland and its immediate neighbour Cumberland, is to describe bleak mountains, extensive wastes and geographical isolation. The territorial divisions created following the Norman Conquest (when these counties were slowly brought under English control) remained more or less relevant into the nineteenth century. These were ancient territories dominated by a few landed magnates. 'Landed' property equated to political power which was brought to bear on dependants and tenants alike.

Beneath the top layer of baronial control were manorial families who usually worked in conjunction with their overlords. This eventually included the Whartons who came to exercise influence in both counties. In Cumberland the principal baronial lords in the west were the families of Percy and Lowther. The Lowther family was further divided into two branches that finally came to merge under Sir James Lowther in the 1750's. The merger created an immensely powerful political force with economic interests in West Cumberland in coal and the development of Whitehaven as a port for foreign trade. There was considerable outward cargo from Whitehaven for the Virginia tobacco trade which benefited inland traders in textiles for example. The political influence of the Lowthers continued throughout the nineteenth century.

Westmorland was a county just over half the size of Cumberland and consisted of two ancient baronies; Westmorland including Appleby Castle and the Barony of Kendal. Westmorland Barony finally came into the hands of the Veteripont family passing through marriage to the Cliffords in the fourteenth century and later, in the seventeenth century, to the Tuftons, earls of Thanet. In the Barony of Kendal one part came finally to be controlled by the Grahams of Levens and the other by the Lowther family. The collapse of the Wharton estate early in the eighteenth century allowed the Lowthers to consolidate their hold in the county. Robert Lowther of Maulds Meaburn bought the Wharton Westmorland estates (including Wharton Hall) and parts of Appleby went to another branch of the family. By the eighteenth century Westmorland came to be dominated politically by the great estates of the Lowthers. Before the Reform Bill of 1832 Appleby had been a rotten borough returning two members of Parliament, normally unopposed Conservatives, and the county returned two more. In spite of further electoral changes and a widening of the franchise with the 1884 Reform Bill it was not until 1900 that an Appleby election was won by a Liberal. At a national level probably the most important event to change this way of life, political domination by wealthy elites, was the First World War. What emerged from the Great War was the Franchise Act of 1918 providing manhood suffrage to Britain along with a restricted franchise for women, extended a decade later.

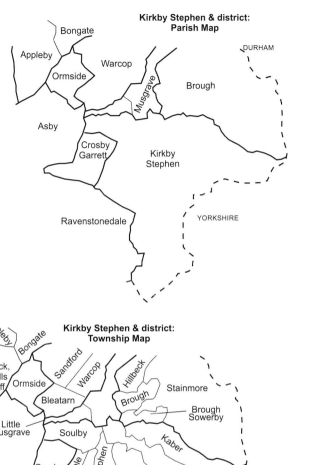

**Kirkby Stephen & district:
Parish Map**

Bongate

Appleby

Ormside

Warcop

Musgrave

Brough

DURHAM

Asby

Crosby
Garrett

Kirkby
Stephen

Ravenstonedale

YORKSHIRE

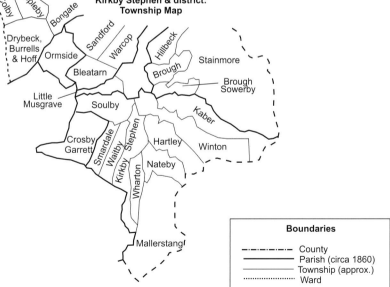

**Kirkby Stephen & district:
Township Map**

Colby

Appleby

Bongate

Sandford

Warcop

Hillbeck

Stainmore

Drybeck,
Burrells
& Hoff

Ormside

Bleatarn

Brough

Brough
Sowerby

Little
Musgrave

Soulby

Kaber

Crosby
Garrett

Smardale

Waitby

Kirkby Stephen

Hartley

Winton

Wharton

Nateby

Mallerstang

Boundaries	
–·–·–·–	County
———	Parish (circa 1860)
———	Township (approx.)
··········	Ward

Chapter 1

Early Settlement

Frank's Bridge: An ancient crossing point prior to the seventeenth century bridge

In writing about the distant past there is a danger of facing what one archaeologist has called *the long silences of prehistory*. We know in outline that Mesolithic hunters inhabited Cumbria some 6,000 years ago and that shortly thereafter Neolithic people were fashioning fine grained stone axe-heads in Lakeland. But how they lived in social and cultural terms remains something of a mystery. In coming to terms with prehistory much of the evidence remains in the landscape. The slow and gradual development of that landscape through time without too much interference means that the archaeological record has remained less subject to disturbance. The ground is littered with potential knowledge: earthworks, field-banks, mills, ancient settlements and pathways although some have subsequently been robbed and re-used. To treat all this chronologically also carries problems because a piece in the jigsaw may often merge with another time period and our terms of reference also continue to evolve and adapt. A case in point occurred in 2010 with an exciting archaeological 'find' on the upland of the Eden valley close to the village of Crosby Garrett near Kirkby Stephen. The discovery of a very unusual and rare bronze Roman cavalry helmet was made by metal detectorists on one of their visits from County Durham. The helmet is believed to have been an item worn by the Roman army on sporting occasions rather than for military use. It could help us understand more about Roman life on the frontier zone of northern England. In terms of craftsmanship the helmet ranks in significance with only a few other similar bronze masterpieces that have been uncovered across the world. The helmet was found buried and in many pieces and raised an intriguing question as to the reasons for its deposition. The find site is now identified as a previously unrecorded village settlement containing Roman and prehistoric remains including a hut circle and earthworks. The find site is some five or six miles from the nearest Roman fort at Brough opening up potentially fresh ways for understanding the relations between 'native' settlements and the Roman army. A later survey revealed earthworks consistent with a village settlement and previous discoveries of Roman coins in the vicinity suggest a Romano-British site. One aspect of this site description includes the likelihood of trading relations between the two cultures which would be consistent with the way the Romans governed their provinces. Whilst the earthworks were previously unrecorded there are many other recorded settlements sites in the wider locality also believed to have been occupied in the Roman period by an indigenous population although very few of these have been excavated.

Left (CH413093): Front left view of the helmet. Constructed in two pieces: a bowl for the rear, sides and top of the head and a mask resembling a human face. Pierced eyes are incorporated in the mask for vision. Other elaborate mask features include a pierced nose, parted lips and rows of curly hair. The components would have been hinged at the top and straps would have secured the front and rear halves. A crest of hair would normally have been worn across the ridge of the helmet.

Right (CH871729): The figure on top of the helmet would have been soldered and features a griffin - a mythical winged and beaked creature with raised feathered wings.

Roman / Private Collection / Photo © Christie's Images / The Bridgeman Art Library

Crosby Garrett Helmet find location site

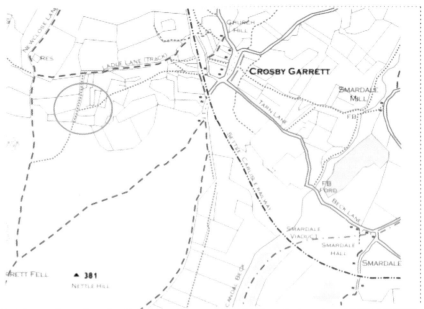

Sketch map based on the Ordnance Survey 1:25000 First Series sheet NY70 (1950/1)

◯ Find location site

The degree of interaction between these two populations during the Roman period has never been fully resolved. The Ewe Close settlement at Crosby Ravensworth, some seven miles west, was excavated in 1907-8 and the main arterial road leading to Hadrian's Wall had been noted to have apparently deviated to pass this site.

In spite of the presence of so much documented Roman activity in the wider area there remains little direct evidence of Roman remains in Kirkby Stephen itself. Even so arguments have been constructed in favour. One of the most intriguing aspects is the location of a Roman fort at Brough-by-Bainbridge in Wensleydale. It seems that this Pennine fort was occupied during most of the Roman period and road communications to it have been inferred in all directions except to the north. This question of Roman routes in the area will be returned to shortly because a direct link with the extensive Roman road network across Stainmore would suggest a possible connection through Mallerstang although this has never been conclusively demonstrated. Another interesting piece of evidence arose with the discovery of the Mallerstang Hoard of Roman coins in 1926. The hoard was discovered by John Kerr, of Mallerstang, concealed in a hole in the ground covered by a stone slab. The 138 coins are dated down to AD 136 - 138. It is not unusual to find hoards in remote places because their deposition is often linked to times of crisis and a need to secure valuables. Early accounts of the find (in 1927) located it at 'Sleddle Mouth' on Mallerstang Edge but it is not clear whether the location site was badly described. Mallerstang Edge even today is difficult of direct access from the valley and the only name now coming close to matching 'Sleddle' is 'Steddale Mouth' located on the Edge between High Seat and Gregory Chapel. Both the first edition six inch Ordnance Survey map of 1861 and modern 1:25000 scale maps identify 'Steddale Mouth' which seems to be the most likely find point. Certainly if this were the remote location of the hoard it would suggest a familiarity with a difficult landscape. Another aspect of Roman activity in the vicinity of Kirkby Stephen is the proliferation of prehistoric or 'Romano-British' sites particularly to the east on the limestone upland between Kirkby Stephen and Shap and, of course, including the recent find of the Crosby Garrett helmet.

Returning to the question of 'Roman roads' in or near Kirkby Stephen this is a topic raised in the book 'Kirkby Stephen' by Anne & Alec Swailes (1985). It explores the possibility of a southern route from Brough-under-Stainmore via the river Belah to Winton, Hartley and Nateby. It is clear that many ancient routes (now bridleways on modern maps) track south on either side of the river Eden.

The Swailes' suggested a continued line south from Nateby somewhere by the modern road (B6259). Another route may have continued on the opposite bank of the river through the site of Wharton Hall to Water Yat at the head of Mallerstang. It seems clear that the shallow river here could have facilitated a crossing to join a much more substantial track running south to the site of Pendragon Castle. Further south again from 'The Thrang' the broad track of the old road or 'The Highway' climbs to cross Hell Gill and continues on a spectacular high level route at 400 metres for another six miles before descending into the head of Cotterdale and Wensleydale.

Another candidate for a Roman route lies adjacent to the A683 Ravenstonedale to Sedbergh

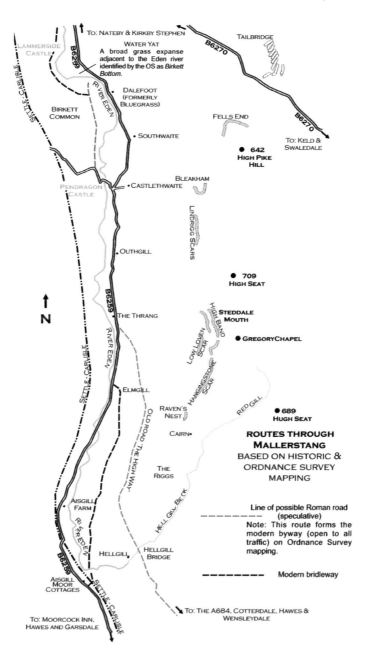

TO: NATEBY & KIRKBY STEPHEN

LAMMERSIDE CASTLE

B6259

WATER YAT
A broad grass expanse adjacent to the Eden river identified by the OS as *Birkett Bottom*.

B6270   TAILBRIDGE

DALEFOOT (FORMERLY BLUEGRASS)

RIVER EDEN

SETTLE - CARLISLE

BIRKETT COMMON

FELLS END

B6270

• SOUTHWAITE

TO: KELD & SWALEDALE

● 642 HIGH PIKE HILL

PENDRAGON CASTLE

BLEAKHAM

• CASTLETHWAITE

LINDRIGG SCARS

• OUTHGILL

● 709 HIGH SEAT

HIGH BAND

STEDDALE MOUTH

↑ N

B6259

• THE THRANG

RIVER EDEN

LOW LOVEN SCAR

● GREGORY CHAPEL

HANGINGSTONE SCAR

RED GILL

● 689 HUGH SEAT

SETTLE - CARLISLE

ELMGILL

OLD ROAD 'THE HIGH WAY'

RAVEN'S NEST

CAIRN •

ROUTES THROUGH
MALLERSTANG
BASED ON HISTORIC & ORDNANCE SURVEY MAPPING

THE RIGGS

• AISGILL FARM

RIVER EDEN

HELLGILL BECK

HELLGILL •   HELLGILL BRIDGE

— — — — —   Line of possible Roman road (speculative)
Note: This route forms the modern byway (open to all traffic) on Ordnance Survey mapping.

B6259

SETTLE - CARLISLE

AISGILL MOOR COTTAGES

— — — — — —   Modern bridleway

TO: MOORCOCK INN, HAWES AND GARSDALE

TO: THE A684, COTTERDALE, HAWES & WENSLEYDALE

road on the minor road through Fell End which descends to the main road at Rawthey Bridge. Habitations here use names such as 'The Street' and 'Street Farm' and as such provide identities often associated with a Roman presence. This old route crosses the river Rawthey and continues over Bluecaster. But in the absence of anything more certain speculation remains a useful alternative for trying to piece together what little we know of some ancient routes. The circumstantial evidence of Romano-British sites and a coin hoard lends some weight to the possibility but until there is more evidence caution is needed.

In later medieval times Stainmore Forest, (originally a hunting forest under baronial control), and the ancient route across the Pass formed a boundary for a wild piece of Pennine upland stretching north to the river Tees and south to the river Swale and remarkable for the vast scale of its landscape and its isolation. From the earliest times we can conjecture that the region had been of strategic importance. Before the Romans it seems that the Stainmore crossing already connected east with west probably from the Neolithic period when the Irish sea enabled communication with other regions of Atlantic Europe. Indeed, there are pre-historic sites at or near the Rey Cross, on Stainmore; a stone circle and the remains of a native settlement on a terrace below the Roman marching camp (discussed shortly). There are various interpretations for the stone circle (also described as a ring cairn or a burial mound) but its dating seems to lie in the late Neolithic or early Bronze age. The stone circle consists of a low mound about 20 metres in diameter. If it is compared with other stone circles in the wider vicinity its significance could lie in being adjacent to this ancient high level route.

The native settlement below the Rey Cross Roman marching camp consists of enclosure walling and mounds of stone possibly of circular house foundations. It has not been dated accurately other than being prehistoric. It seems to have been occupied over a long period but may have been used only seasonally.

The A66 high level trunk road from the A1 at Scotch Corner traverses west to Brough under Stainmore. The modern line overlays much of the original Roman route and the Stainmore Pass itself forms part of a strategic network of roads and forts laid down by the Romans. This network underlined the importance of this east-west transverse route across the Pennine chain of northern England. In discussing the Roman interlude Stainmore therefore forms a central part of any account of Roman activity.

Indeed, Stainmore is significant for two reasons. Firstly, there are a variety of archaeological remains in the vicinity including those on the Stainmore Pass itself. Secondly, some of these remains can still be visited largely because of their very remoteness and isolation. Even the earliest modern travellers seem to have hastened through this inhospitable area and today the Lake District remains a far greater attraction for many visitors to Cumbria. There may be potentially richer sites in the wider area but searching for them is difficult and many may already have been destroyed or at least disturbed by later agricultural activity. It is ironic that much of the recent archaeological investigation has taken place on Stainmore as a result of the encroachment of the modern A66 road into the delicate fabric of this upland area. But the effect has been to stimulate the need to sift and interpret evidence about some sites whose origins, in some cases, lie millennia in the past. There is also now an increasing awareness of the importance of prehistoric activity in upland areas of Britain which the specialists are beginning to recognise. Pollen sampling confirms that peat deposits in the uplands started to form during the fourth millennium BC and the area of Stainmore and Bowes Moor was no exception in supporting mixed woodland up to the later part of the same period. This is referred to as natural wildwood which covered, in various forms, most parts of the British Isles before the start of large scale human activity. It is probable that by the time of the arrival of the Romans on Stainmore this woodland had disappeared.

The most significant field monuments on Stainmore lie in County Durham just across the Cumbria boundary (the old county of Westmorland). These consist of a pre-Norman boundary stone called the Rey Cross and what is claimed as a Roman marching camp known by the same name

Rey Cross is a pre-Norman boundary stone erected about 950AD marking the border between the Scottish kingdom of Strathclyde and English Northumbria. The cross originally stood within the Roman camp to the west but was re-sited in a lay-by when the A66 was widened. The remaining weathered stump is the top section and is all that survives although originally it would have been three metres in height with carved decorations. Another variant on its origin is that it marks the burial site of Erik Bloodaxe, the last Viking ruler of York who was killed nearby. However, recent excavation has yielded no evidence for a grave. Until recently the cross marked the boundary between the old counties of Westmorland and the North Riding of Yorkshire.

The earliest account we have about them was written in the sixteenth century when they were described by John Leland, a pioneer of direct enquiry and observation. His original intention had been to survey the libraries of the soon to be dissolved monasteries in the reign of Henry VIII. In the process he became fascinated about recording 'a hole World of Thinges very memorable'. A later and romantic description was made in the seventeenth century by William Camden who drew on Leland's manuscripts for topographical detail. Camden was particularly interested in reconstructing Roman Britain using the title *Britannia* for his publication. Camden described the road into Westmorland laying right across Stainmore 'entirely desolate and solitary, except one inn in the middle for the entertainment of travellers'. This would seem to be the first reference to the Old Spital Inn. Nothing now remains of this medieval building where farm buildings initially from the eighteenth century now occupy the site.

An accurate survey of the two monuments was made by General Roy in 1793 and following this very little was done in the Victorian period. The next detailed assessment was made by two archaeologists, Richmond and McIntyre, whose work is now seen to be foundational for the subsequent exploration of a chain of possible Roman signalling stations connecting, at the least, the Roman forts at Bowes and Brough.

The badly eroded stump of Rey Cross, Stainmore Pass from an early photograph by Elijah Yeoman c.1900. The stump remains today next to a layby on the A66(T).

© The Bowes Museum

The Upper Eden Valley in Roman Times

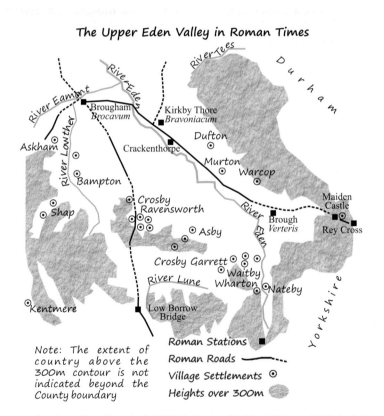

Note: The extent of country above the 300m contour is not indicated beyond the County boundary

Roman Stations ■
Roman Roads ——— - - -
Village Settlements ⊙
Heights over 300m

From the map *Roman Westmorland* in RCHM: An Inventory of the Historical Monuments in Westmorland. HMSO, 1936.

As discussed the route laid down so accurately across Stainmore by the Romans is followed more or less by the modern A66 road. It leaves Scotch Corner to cross undulating lowland pasture and then climbs slowly to over 400 metres before descending to Brough in the Eden Valley and continuing west to Penrith. There are other east-west transverse routes across northern England; in Weardale to the north and further south in Swaledale but these would have been longer routes and probably less hospitable (even than Stainmore !). Later, in the Domesday Survey of 1086 Swaledale was described as waste although, like Stainmore, it was used for hunting in the medieval period. W G Hoskins in *The Making of the English Landscape* suggests that as late as the 1790's three quarters of Westmorland remained uncultivated. A network of forts was eventually created between the Roman centre of York and Carlisle. The city of York was founded by the ninth legion of the Roman army in AD71 when a fortress was established on the banks of the river Ouse. A civilian settlement or vicus developed probably in the second century to become one of the most important towns of Roman Britain. Forts were established on the western route to Carlisle at Bowes, Brough, Kirkby Thore and Brougham near Penrith. This strategic network formed part of the frontier zone of northern England. Further north Hadrian's Wall was constructed as a continuous barrier between Tyne and Solway. The Wall was planned by the Emperor Hadrian during a visit to Britain in AD122.

One 'problem' of Hadrian's Wall today lies in understanding how it was pieced together because its structure was altered even whilst it was being built. There are still many aspects of Roman activity for which there is insufficient evidence to make firm conclusions. In the same way the 'evidence' for the Stainmore signal system, referred to shortly, continues to be a subject for discussion and interpretation.

Certainly, there is more information about Hadrian's Wall but our understanding about its purpose has altered over time. Originally the Wall tended to be regarded as purely defensive but more recent research has viewed it as a mechanism for controlling and regulating the flow of traffic from one side to the other.

Hadrian's Wall took advantage of natural features for example by keeping to high ground. It replaced an earlier network of forts in the valley bottom just to the south on what is called the *Stanegate*. One of these original forts which preceded the Wall proper was *Vindolanda* in the central section close to Corbridge. It is at *Vindolanda* that since the 1970's a large number of documents have been unearthed which have provided new evidence of the day to day life of a Roman frontier garrison. The documents are texts written on small sheets of wood. Hundreds have been recovered and many contain the minutia of Roman daily life; for example personal accounts and letters. It has provided a fresh stimulus to reassessing our understanding of the social and domestic connections underpinning military life.

The Roman fort *Verterae* at Church Brough was strategically situated on the trans-Pennine route linking the western approach to Brougham and Carlisle via the Lune valley (passing Ewe Close at Crosby Ravensworth) and the route from Brougham to Stainmore. This transverse route was also significant in connecting the south of the frontier zone with the Stanegate and Hadrian's Wall. Both Brough and Kirkby Thore were permanent garrisons.

Verterae measures approximately 400x250 feet but otherwise its structure is only known through literature and chance discoveries. Indications from coins and pottery suggest occupation began in the first century under the Flavians and continued to the late fourth century. The relative significance of the Stainmore Pass is its identification with a signalling system which may have formed part of the network of Roman frontier forts in lowland Scotland and the Pennines.

The Roman fort at Brough defended the strategic military highway connecting the base fortress of York with Brougham and Carlisle in the west. From the east the modern A66 follows the course of the Roman road for much of the journey from Scotch Corner to Stainmore. However the modern route passes through the southern edge of Market Brough, a settlement created later than Church Brough where Verterae is sited. The original line of the Roman road leaves the A66 at Banks Gate (GR 845148) about 3 miles east of Brough and only re-joins it about 2 miles west of the town. The OS 1:25000 map labels the minor road as Roman and the earlier six inch OS sheet (xvi, SE) shows a small section as the Maiden Way just west of Leonard's Cragg. The Roman line continues south of Augill Castle through broken country but the exact route still requires identification - see sketch map below. It is thought that a short branch road would have been needed to connect the east gate of the fort with this road.

Maiden Castle, a Roman fortlet situated close to the summit of the Stainmore pass and above

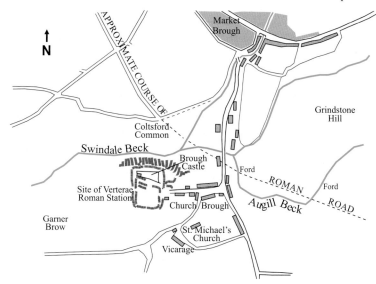

Sketch map of the approximate course of the Roman road as it traverses Verterae Roman station at Brough. NOTE: The map is based on a drawing made circa 1958 and does not depict the modern A66(T) which passes just south of Market Brough nor the A685 which by-passed Church Brough on its eastern side.

Source: Eric Birley. 'The Roman fort at Brough-under-Stainmore'. CW2, lviii.

the modern A66 road, is dated from the second century. It commands a strategic position overlooking the Eden valley and lies in full view of *Verterae* at Brough. Maiden Castle has been extensively robbed of stone although sufficient remains to indicate that it was defended by a substantial wall. There have been other disturbances and a carefully paved pack-horse track is also thought to cut through the fortlet. Pottery and coin finds suggest that it was occupied from the mid second to the late fourth centuries. There are also banked enclosures and possible cultivation plots suggesting settlements that are contemporary with the fortlet. However, visibility from Maiden Castle east to Bowes Moor is obstructed. It has been suggested that there may have been a communications link between the Roman forts of Bowes and Church Brough using a chain of signal stations. Acrucial link in this chain is believed to be Roper Castle. The original work for this proposal was made by the archaeologist I.A.Richmond who suggested an extensive network of stations between York and Stanwix on Hadrian's Wall. Whilst this has not been fully demonstrated there have been finds of other stations or sites east of Brough at Johnson's Plain, Punchbowl Inn and Augill Bridge close to the A66. Although in this context the exact line of the original Roman road did not seem to follow the modern A66 at these points. The excavations give credence to a possible signal network between Bowes and Church Brough. Roper Castle is situated at an unusual location on wet, boggy ground one mile south west of Bowes Moor. This location facilitates a visual link between the two fortlets of Bowes Moor and Maiden Castle. Research has continued with aerial photography and excavation to piece together the possibility of a signal network although problems of authentication remain. The use of the term 'tower' instead of 'signal station' has also been proposed. The 'towers' have been noted elsewhere but doubts about their function remain. They may have been constructed when the future of Roman Britain was under threat but, on the other hand, there is no record of 'signalling' as a function within the Roman army nor any evidence that anyone at these Stainmore posts were capable of being supported in this specific role.

Finally, Rey Cross camp on the Stainmore Pass further east on the A66 is the site of a Roman marching camp. The Rey Cross camp or temporary marching base is compared to another great earthwork at Crackenthorpe in the Eden valley. The Rey Cross camp was slightly smaller (about 20 acres) and the two were sixteen miles apart inviting speculation that both were used either by early Roman invaders or Roman engineers building roads once conquest was secure. Rey Cross camp lies at the very summit of the Stainmore Pass at 1480 feet. It seems that the camp may have preceded the road whilst at Crackenthorpe the reverse applies.

The Rey Cross work has been dated to the first century suggesting a possible use for a first Roman invasion of Cumbria. One commentator has suggested that a more confident unit would have been unlikely to have camped in such an inhospitable location!

The area had to be brought under direct Roman control after the collapse of the Brigantian administration of this northern frontier zone. This had happened because the Brigantian queen, Cartimandua, was overthrown by internal opposition. At this point the Roman governor of Britain, Petillius Cerealis, intervened militarily. It is possible that the Rey Cross camp was created by his army during the first northern campaign to provide temporary accomodation.

There are alternative explanations which favour a later chronology. Recent excavation has been unable to provide conclusive evidence but some of the pottery finds indicate a first century date as does the structure of the camp's layout.

The Roman fort, *Verterae*, occupies the same site as the medieval castle. The name *Verterae* is thought to mean 'summit' and is preserved in Roman documents which relate to military details of the fourth or fifth century. A Roman garrison unit was stationed at the fort and was called *Numerus Directorum* and consisted of three or four hundred auxiliary, part mounted troops.

The fort covers an area of about three acres and much greater than the area occupied by the medieval castle. The fort has been overlaid by the medieval structure but the western rampart is still distinguishable. No internal buildings are visible but excavations beneath the castle keep in 1923 found traces of buildings consistent with a Roman origin.

Verterae is set on an elevated mound overlooking the Swindale beck to the north. Significant archaeological material has emerged from this valley, particularly in the period 1820-60, when the beck eroded a Roman rubbish tip. In fact Roman remains were mixed with those of later periods given that the medieval castle was occupied for many centuries. Among the Roman finds were gold, silver and (mainly) brass coins, bronze objects and a large quantity of lead seals. Inscribed stones have also been discovered, one during the restoration of the south porch of Brough church in 1879.

Coin finds from Brough recorded by the British Museum from 1865 suggest occupation of the site begins under the Flavian emperors (Vespasian AD69-79, Titus AD79-81, Domitian AD81-96) continuing into the late fourth century. Many other coin finds are unrecorded.

Anglo-Saxon settlement in the Eden Valley began in the seventh century with the creation of farmsteads later to become villages such as Dufton, Hilton and Murton. From the late eighth century the area was colonised by Scandinavians from when comprehensive settlement of Westmorland including Stainmore probably began. It is intriguing that a Viking age silver hoard was found by a metal detector in the area of Rey Cross. The hoard consists of silver ingots and a fragment of a silver bracelet all of which have been dated as tenth century. In the parish church of St. Stephen in Kirkby Stephen there is part of an Anglo-Danish or Norse cross shaft known as the Loki stone. It was Norse settlers who so named the town - a drawing of the stone is reproduced in the chapter that follows.

By the ninth century Cumbria was under Scots control from Carlisle. The eastern border with England was close to the summit of Stainmore probably marked by the Rey Cross. English control was only finally established in 1092 by the Normans with the border set at the Solway and from this period the border was defended although incursions continued up to the fourteenth century and beyond.

Following their invasion the Normans re-built many towns and villages and were responsible for the construction of Brough Castle on the site of the Roman fort. The earliest portion of St Michael's church is also Norman and the town of Church Brough seems to have been planned in conjunction with these buildings. (Market Brough was only established later, in the thirteenth century.)

Brough Castle is set on the northern part of the Roman fort and is, as already mentioned, of Norman origin. It consists of a three storey keep - its oldest part built after 1174 - and attendant buildings. The south and west sides of the keep are exterior and form part of the castle's defensive curtain. The keep has a basement and three floors with walls ten feet thick at the base. The main entrance has a flight of exterior steps rising twelve feet from the ground giving access to the first floor. The entrance arch has gone but in Buck's drawing of 1739 it is evident. The remaining buildings consist of a gatehouse in the middle of the south curtain with hall and stables to left and right. Drawing rooms extend into the drum tower known as Clifford's Tower at the south east corner.

The architectural history of Brough Castle and its states of destruction, restoration and repair are not easy to document precisely. The strategic nature of the Stainmore road, Scots incursions in this border region and the unfortunate history of the Barony of Brough in the first half of the fourteenth century all count towards a story of neglect. The Norman keep was probably the first structure in masonry with remaining defenses in timber but the true dimensions of the exterior are unknown.

Probably the first stone Norman building was dismantled by the Scots in 1174 with restoration and further disrepair setting in by 1245. Control of Brough by the important Clifford family began in the later thirteenth century. Its strategic significance involved the castle in the Plantaganet wars with Scotland in the fourteenth century. The lack of a resident proprietor through long periods also contributed to its neglect. The castle was organised more effectively during the rule of Roger, ninth Lord Clifford between 1352 and 1389 when re-building took place. But this was undone in 1521 when a fire destroyed all timber and lead and reduced the building to a skeleton. This damage was only restored in 1659-62, by Lady Anne Clifford, who is credited with the restoration of much that was destroyed. Considerable damage had also been done during the Civil War.

Lady Ann's daughter and heiress, Margaret, took the Clifford estates, including Brough, to the Tufton family from when, with the exception of Appleby Castle, they fell into decay. By 1695 stones from Brough were used for repairs at Appleby. In 1714 the fittings at Brough were sold and further neglect continued until part of the keep collapsed in 1792.

The early history of the Parish Church of St Michael is also sparse but its origin may be consistent with the castle. The Norman work is thought to be of two periods. An early Norman structure may have been destroyed dating the earliest work in the present church, on the south wall, to the middle or late eleventh century with some further work at the end of the Norman period. One dating suggests that the whole south wall of the nave is Norman with one plain Norman window in the west most bay belonging to the earlier period. The church was re-built at least twice during the later Middle Ages and further reconstruction in the sixteenth century including the addition of the western tower.

To the Right Hon:
Sackvile Tufton Earl of Thanet
Baron Tufton Lord Westmorland & Vesey Lord of Skipton in
Craven & Hereditary Sheriff of the County of Westmorland

Burgh or **Brough** Castle under Staine more, was casually
consumed by Fire A.D.1521, and was rebuilt A.D.1661 by the
Lady Anne Clifford, Countess Dowager of Pembroke & sole
Daughter & Heir of George Clifford, third Earl of Cumberland
after having lain one hundred and forty years desolate - The
present Proprietor is Right Hon the Earl of Thanet -

The drawing of The South East view of Brough Castle
Samuel & Nathaniel Buck, 1739

In the context of Stainmore and its forest it is useful to distinguish between the word Forest against forest or forestry. This distinction was important in the medieval period when Stainmore Forest formed part of a network of such areas across the upland. In *A History of the Countryside* Oliver Rackham notes that Forest was a place of deer not of trees. A Forest could be wooded but did not need to be whereas a forest was more properly connected with trees. The term *Forest* is thought to originate in the time of William the Conqueror as a legal term referring, as in the case of Stainmore, either to a royal forest or private chase (normally under lordly control). It was unfenced and probably contained both red and roe deer which could be hunted under certain conditions. Stainmore was private chase rather than a royal forest eventually

The modern ruin of Brough Castle

coming under the control of the Clifford family, earls of Cumberland. By the fifteenth century these upland areas whilst remaining under the jurisdiction of baronial lords would have yielded income from letting for grazing rather than being used for private hunting. In the medieval period it was the monasteries that altered much of the landscape of northern England through sheep farming. The transformation of the moorlands proper was, however, more the labour of peasant communities than the monastic orders. The upland also supported a network of tracks. Tan Hill, south east of Stainmore, was an important centre and a focus for coal mining from at least the thirteenth century. Swaledale also became a significant lead mining area with transport connections north to Barnard Castle and Bowes and further south into Yorkshire. Old drove roads also linked Tan Hill with Westmorland, Yorkshire and beyond. This network of tracks facilitated the development of trade in basic commodities from the activities of both mining and agriculture. A complex network of drove roads enabled the long distance transport of cattle.

The Drove Roads map illustrates the dense network of such ancient pathways which fan out into the broad expanse of Yorkshire. Their origin is uncertain but believed to extend back in time to the Neolithic when livestock would most probably have been moved over higher ground in search of new pasture. The droving heyday occurred from the seventeenth to the nineteenth centuries when the economy emerged from medieval stagnation and Scots cattle was moved to southern markets and cattle were fattened en route. Droving eventually came to form a distinctive part of commercial life. The trajectory of the droving trade was distinctively south and west heading initially for the fairs and larger towns. In our case Mallerstang provides a useful reminder of these ancient routes. From Kirkby Stephen one route passed south through Mallerstang with the option to branch east at High Shaw Paddock towards Dent and Thornton in Lonsdale. The alternative was to traverse the old road known as 'The Highway' on a spectacular high level track to Wensleydale. Today some of the ruinous droving inns remain such as High Dike along with many former accomodation fields or 'closes' used to provide temporary pasture for livestock.

Drove Roads of Westmorland & North Yorkshire
A dense network of drove roads trending south

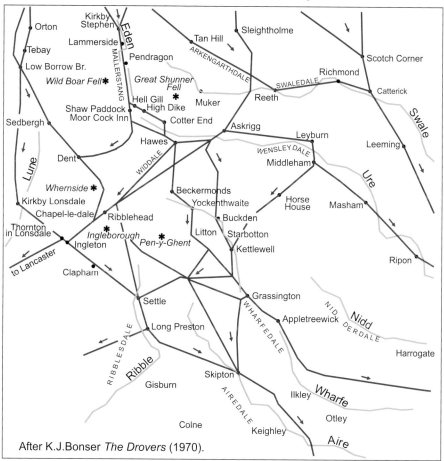

After K.J.Bonser *The Drovers* (1970).

Chapter 2

The Anglo-Scottish Border

*A quiet corner at St. Stephen's Parish Church,
Kirkby Stephen.*

No account of life in a Border community would be complete without a description of the obligations laid upon its inhabitants and in this respect Kirkby Stephen was no exception. John Breay in *Light in the Dales* expressed it well:

> *There were the days when harsh tidings came up the dale, when every man had to obey the call of the Lord Warden of the Marches, put on his war gear, his leather boots, steel cap and jacket, sling his bag of arrows on his back, and with bill, sword or bow set out with every man aged sixteen to sixty to defend the Borders against the raiding Scots. They had to serve on the Borders for fourteen days, with two to come and two to go.*

However before an outline of Border history in this chapter it is useful to be reminded of the significance of Hadrian's Wall in the context of what is now called by historians the *frontier zone* of Roman northern England. This perimeter zone embraced the network of roads and forts discussed in the previous chapter and included the transverse Pennine route from York across Stainmore to Brough and beyond. There is no question that Carlisle is the *Luguvallium* of the Romans even though the line of the wall is no longer visible through the city. But it is a commonplace to note that at every excavation in Carlisle items of Roman make are discovered. Two thousand years later we still acknowledge the Border even though the defining boundaries between the kingdoms of Scotland and England have altered somewhat. Carlisle has been the capital of this Borderland since Roman times at least on the English side and continued to serve a historic role as a garrison town.

Strictly speaking Kirkby Stephen was positioned on the southern extremity of the Borderland but in times of need military support was drawn from the town and its surrounding farms and townships. It also suffered raids by marauding Scots. Kirkby Stephen was by no means a garrison town and there is no comparison with Carlisle in this respect but a look at its layout illustrates a strong element of planning to restrict access to raiders trying to gain entry in earlier centuries. A sketch of the town from the Ordnance Survey sheet of 1862 shows the strategic points (now traffic bottlenecks) which could be defended. The *narrows* in the town remain (on the main street at North Road and the entrance to High Street) as do the high walls that still encircle parts of the old town for example on Stoneshot leading down to Frank's Bridge and Faraday Road (Back Lane as it was called). The narrow on Silver Street was widened in the 1960's (see photograph) when the building on the north west corner was demolished.

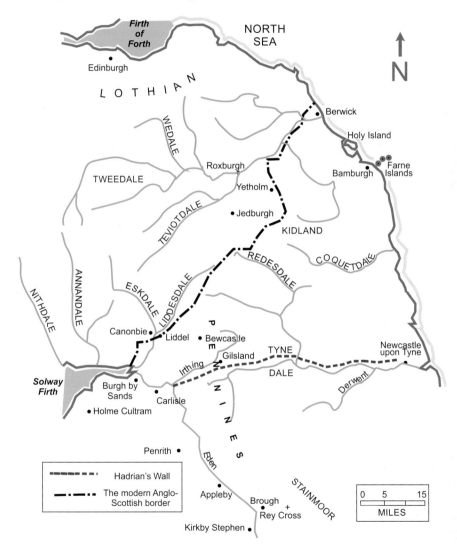

The Anglo-Scottish Border

Two views of Silver Street circa 1910.

Top: *The corner shop was Hayton's confectioners and tea room and was demolished in the 1960's to widen one of the "narrows" in the town.*

Bottom: *Looking east towards the Parish Church.*

High walls and narrow passageways are a feature of Kirkby Stephen's early town boundaries.
***Top:** Little Wiend connecting Market Street with Melbecks.* ***Below:** Faraday Road.*

In Kirkby Stephen, Croft Street connects Market Street with Faraday Road (formerly Back Lane).

The Anglo-Scottish Border provides one context for the network of obligation in these isolated dale communities. The baronial lords and gentry provided the recruitment pool for selection by the king to the positions of Lord and Deputy Warden of the March. In Kirkby Stephen this included the Clifford, Wharton and Musgrave families. The town formed part of the barony of Westmorland held eventually by the Clifford family and based at Appleby Castle. By the seventeenth century the Musgrave and Wharton families had significant land holdings in the town. By the eighteenth century the Wharton estate had passed to the Lowther family (earls of Lonsdale). In the nineteenth century the Clifford estates passed to Lord Hothfield. The fortunes of Sir Thomas, later first Lord, Wharton are closely connected with the military administration of the Border during the sixteenth century and eventually he became a Lord Warden of the March. The other side to the military obligation imposed on the community had been the development of customary tenant right. Tenant right gave rights of inheritance over property which was linked to the obligation imposed on tenants to provide military service on the border. There was also the feature of *fines* imposed when either tenants changed or when there was a change of lord. Later these conditions gave greater security to tenants through to the nineteenth century and helped to underpin the independence and relative freedoms of the peasant community.

The medieval institution of the Border constituted a frontier between two kingdoms and formed the basis for disputes that were invariably settled by violence. Even after a frontier line had been established there were areas that remained *debateable land*. There were few full scale battles in the border region but one fight did occur on the Solway Moss in 1542 which helped gain Sir Thomas Wharton's elevation to the peerage as one of Henry VIII`s *new men*. Geographically, the Solway Mosses are as remote from the centre of English government as is possible and were also at the western edge of the long border conflict. Much of the conflict was not political or territorial but just family feuding, cattle stealing and plunder accompanied by brutality and blackmail. The mosses were in fact a place of sanctuary where pursuit was difficult. The border reivers held sway over this lawless no man's land for over four hundred years throughout much of the Middle Ages.

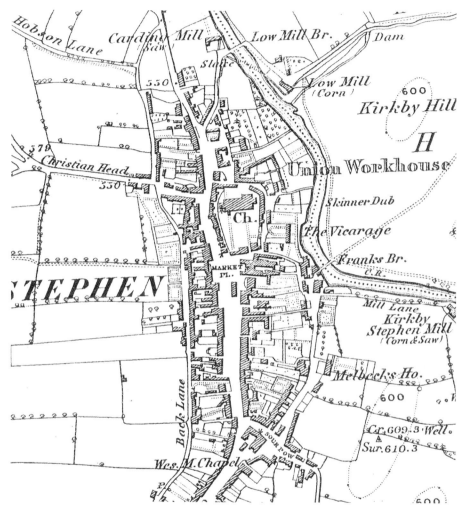

Kirkby Stephen from the first edition six inch to one mile Ordnance Survey sheet XXIII East Ward, 1862.
The map illustrates the "narrows" and the defensible extremities leading into the town. The areas around
the church and Market Place would seem to have potential for accommodating people and livestock when
necessary. Note Silver Street continues east from Christian Head towards the main street and the church.

Not to scale

Cumbria Archive Service. Kendal.

The lawlessness was only finally resolved with the Union of Crowns between Scotland and England in 1603 under the Stuart James VI (Scotland) and I (England) and in 1707 when the border ceased to separate two independent kingdoms.

As already mentioned in the more distant past Hadrian's Wall provided a permanent physical reminder of a frontier division. Some historians write of *the strange peace of the post-Roman centuries* when Roman order dissolved. In spite of attacks on England's shores even during the last years of the Roman Empire any sense of security was destroyed by the Viking attack on Lindisfarne in AD 793. The Vikings had an enormous impact thereafter. It was Norse settlers who so named Kirkby Stephen. The Loki Stone, a pre-Conquest stone depicting a bound figure from Norse mythology, remains in St. Stephen's church and is thought to date to early in the eleventh century. It was not until William of Normandy conquered England in 1066, later dealing ruthlessly with the northern territory, that a long process of border pacification began.

Part of an Anglo-Danish or Norse cross-shaft known as the Loki Stone or Bound Man Devil at St. Stephen's Church, Kirkby Stephen.

Reproduced from CW1, VII, 1884.

Before the Normans the former kingdom of Cumbria had been contested territory whose possession passed between England, Northumbria, Strathclyde and Scotland. Even at the Domesday Survey it seems that the Eden valley and most of Cumberland was probably not regarded as part of England. The territory continued to be contested even after the Normans. William Rufus finally captured Carlisle to create an English colony in 1092. The east of the country remained under Scots control as far west as Gilsland. English control was only finally established under Henry II in 1157 although the Border as such between Tweed and Solway was only confirmed around the middle of the thirteenth century. The settlement involved a loss to Scotland of Berwick in the east.

There is no exact chronology of how Cumbria came to be brought into the Norman administration of England but the roots probably reach back to the eleventh century. There is one Ivo Taillebois who, with his wife, jointly formed a Benedictine priory in Lincolnshire. Taillebois subsequently acquired jurisdiction in both Cumberland and Westmorland. There is documentary evidence that he presented five parish churches and half his demesne of Kirkby Stephen, and its church, to the newly established St Mary's Abbey in York. By 1122 Ranulph Meschin was Lord from Solway to Derwent based at Appleby. About this time a decision was made to make Carlisle a strategic stronghold with a Norman castle and a cathedral although this newly acquired Borderland held strong Scottish sympathies and traditions. The Norman strategy was to encourage occupation by Anglo-Norman families, such as Taillebois, along with the establishment of monasteries. Gilsland was held by the Scots and was eventually wrested from them by Hubert de Vaux. Lanercost Priory, in the heart of Gilsland, was created by Hubert's son Robert in about 1169 but it remained vulnerable to raiding parties from over the border.

The feudal system was gradually introduced by the Anglo-Norman overlords but the old culture of clans and chieftains was never entirely displaced and ancient tribal loyalty endured even beyond the eventual union of both kingdoms. Up to the end of the thirteenth century there were acts of barbarity on both sides when property, including churches and monasteries, suffered and individual life held small value. But it could be said that the twelfth and thirteenth centuries were reasonably peaceful by medieval standards. A new era opened after the death of Alexander III in 1285. Scotland developed a strong sense of independence and, in England, there was a growing awareness of Scotland's strategic importance and this nurtured a sense of anxiety. One solution, both obvious and impossible, was to bring Scotland under English control and the next few hundred years reflect attempts to achieve this goal. At the same time Scotland cultivated its relations with France. It became a tradition that when England embarked on military expeditions on the continent the Scots invaded the north of England often with French encouragement.

During the reign of Edward I relations deteriorated and whilst the institutions for civil order remained in place many of the inhabitants of the border region learnt a lawless self sufficiency which valued self-interest over the restraints of central authority. It is from this era that the fourteenth, fifteenth and sixteenth centuries can be characterised by chronic warfare and devastation. The first Lord Wharton was involved in that last century, the sixteenth, before the process of border pacification commenced.

With the militarisation of the Border came the creation of a Border land. Warfare continued inexorably. There was Scots success at Bannockburn (1314) and regular incursions south sometimes reaching as far as Yorkshire and Westmorland. Cattle and prisoners were taken and Appleby burned. Later border reivers were to learn the methods of blackmail and protection from the indemnities imposed on the English. A settled way of life became impossible and taught border inhabitants how to fight for survival. This state of affairs continued until the end of the sixteenth century although lawlessness continued after this time.

Related to the Border was its defence. Border tenant right had developed as a form of tenure granted to men in the isolated communities of the north for defending the country against the Scots. It certainly applied in Westmorland but its origins are unclear. Whilst related to border duties some writers have seen it emerging from the free settlements established by the Vikings. Other accounts suggest it existed as northern customary tenure in Northumbria and was never completely absorbed by Norman feudalism. Its duties obliged men aged sixteen to sixty to serve on the border. The length of service may have varied through time but by the sixteenth century it was probably for fourteen days with two additional days for travel each way. Tenant land was occupied by tenure originally founded on border service but later commuted to fixed money payments as ancient rent. All these and other forms of servitude were finally absorbed into customary tenure and tenant right within the manorial system. Perhaps by the fourteenth century tenants had a right for their children to inherit their land or sell it. On the other hand by the sixteenth century there were many disputes between lord and tenant due to inflation and the rapacity of some lords. Disputes often occurred over rents and the fines charged at the death of a lord or a change of tenant.

A distinct law for Border administration developed as rules of the Lords Wardens of the Marches during the reign of Edward I. The first such Lord Warden of the English March was Robert de Clifford appointed in 1296. The Cliffords came from the Welsh March and aspired to the barony of Westmorland as hereditary Sheriffs. Robert lost his life at Bannockburn. The Border itself was divided into three sectors - the West March of Cumberland, Middle and East Marches of Northumberland. Service varied over time but generally the Warden would adjudicate disputes through courts and sessions during periods of truce with their counterparts on the other side of the Border - the Scottish Marches and their wardens, deputies and serjeants. March law was binding and intended to provide conditions for settling disputes over a wide range of activities that disturbed the peace including murder, wounding, fire raising, theft, deadly feud or forms of trespass in the opposing realm such as tree felling and hunting. The pursuit of hot trod was considered legitimate for the Warden of either kingdom to pursue and apprehend fugitives *with hand and horn, with hue and cry, unto such time and place as the fugitive or offender be apprehended, and to bring them again within their own jurisdiction.* Traditionally, the role of warden was occupied by individuals drawn from the ranks of the few noble families with sufficient power and status to manage the role. These were such English dynasties as Clifford, Dacre, Neville and Percy all major northern landowners and capable of securing cooperation from their tenants through the exercise of patronage and obligation. There were instances later, particularly in the sixteenth century, of other appointees being unable to perform the warden's role effectively due to lack of experience or support in the region. On the other hand the powerful nobles were both capable of disobedience to the crown and of disagreeing between themselves. Feuding between noble families was also a feature of border life as much as it was between rival clans. It is, indeed, appropriate to comment that the magnates were sometimes both duplicitous in encouraging lawlessness and acted in the same way themselves.

It was in these circumstances that Henry VIII, for example, on occasion chose to prefer 'new men' to take responsibility because they were potentially able to offer greater loyalty and obedience to the crown. Thomas, first Lord Wharton was one example. At the same time one historian of the March has described Thomas Wharton as one of the most expert borderers. The focus of the western march in north Cumberland, a strategic hub of the border region, were the river valleys of Annan, Kirktle, Esk, Liddel, Irthing and Eden all of which converge on the Solway Firth north of Carlisle. This area included the Debateable Lands of the Solway Moss which, until the process of pacification began later in the sixteenth century, had been a source of tension between Border lawlessness and attempts at settled farming. It was a militarised frontier with constant raiding across the Border for cattle, sheep and other plunder. The Marches contained two garrisoned towns; Berwick and Carlisle and the region was also defended by

A The Castle.
B Cathedral Church of St. Mary.
C Church of St. Cuthbert.
D The Market Place.
E The Citadel.

CARLISLE
in the reign of
QUEEN ELIZABETH

Scale of Feet.
50 100   200   300   400   500   600

Reproduced from *Historic Towns: Carlisle.* M. Creighton. Longmans, Green & Co. London (1889).

other royal and baronial castles. However, apart from the lawless zone astride the frontier much of the remainder of northern England was integrated into national political life and civil society.

The process of pacifying the Border ended a centuries old problem and became one of the achievements of the Stuart monarchy. The old way of life was slowly altered with the establishment of law and order and civil administration although it did not happen overnight. In north Cumberland, the West March where the first Lord Wharton initially served, there continued to be trouble spots where three Crown properties lay adjacent to the frontier - Bewcastle, Nichol Forest and the English Debateable Lands. During the sixteenth century the leading West March clan were the Grahams. They had spread across the border to the English side and dominated other borderers in and around the crown estates. They grew more powerful and by the end of the century became an unmatched Border defence force. Their overlords were the Scotts of Buccleuch. As reivers they were a permanent danger to more peaceful neighbours and outnumbered existing English borderers. Thomas, Lord Wharton had commented in 1548 that the Debateable Lands were comparable with other fertile land in the north but the area was characterised by poor land use, poverty and under-employment. The pressure to occupy more land had occurred because of a growing population and had not met with resistance because of the absence of regulation.

The transitional period for the gradual change in Border policy which culminated in the accession of James VI to the English throne was extremely complex. The Tudor government had preferred to limit their commitment to providing border defence and had relied more on wardens and their borderers. At the same time a new warden, Lord Scrope, had insufficient authority to impose control. Like some other 'new men' he had proved to be ill suited to coping with the intricate politics of the border clans, particularly the Grahams. The crown was also a major absentee landowner on the Border and depended on local men to administer their estates but who also remained independent of wardens who were nominally responsible for royal property. A further vacuum was created by a non-resident land owning nobility who also used local nominees to manage their affairs and in turn perpetuated feuds and quarrels within the border area. The warden was expected to manage these exclusive interests including containing the potential violence of the Grahams who had been favoured by previous governments and continued to be treated leniently believing they contributed to order. The question of the removal of troublesome clans out of the area, including transportation abroad, had been suggested but never acted upon. Various incidents illustrate the incapacity of Lord Scrope but show some of the mystique and romance of the border reiver. In the Border ballads there is a strong oral tradition of folk poetry which celebrates the bleak realism of their way of life.

Within this system of kinship allegiance to a family surname on either side of the border invariably retained prior claim over any higher political authority. Sir Walter Scott (1771-1832) was a descendant of a famous Border clan and he collected many of the ballads which were published as The Minstrelsy of the Scottish Borders in 1802.

The Ballad of Kinmont Willie celebrates the audacious rescue of Willie Armstrong from Scrope's headquarters at Carlisle Castle in 1596 by Sir Walter Scott of Buccleuch with Graham help. Willie had been captured on a day of truce for an offence in Bewcastle but there was already animosity between Buccleuch and Lord Scrope. It was an incident which seriously offended Queen Elizabeth. Over a year later the leading Grahams were brought before the Privy Council but were again treated leniently and Scrope reprimanded for not providing sufficient evidence against them. The Carlisle Treaty of 1597 placed wider constraint on border clans although it proved to be ineffective initially but after 1603 the gentry were incorporated into local administration with Border Councils in each March. Another step towards normalisation occurred when two major troublemakers of the Scottish clans, Sir Walter Scott and Sir Robert Ker of Cesford were removed away from the Border to England in 1597/8. Greater cooperation between Scotland and England did eventually yield results. Audacious incidents continued however. In 1600 Wattie Graham, accused of stealing a horse in Westmorland from Thomas Salkeld - a member of the gentry - was due to appear at Appleby but other Grahams kidnapped Salkeld's six year old son and returned to Scotland. Lord Scrope was obliged to release Wattie to get the boy back. These incidents probably helped to cement relationships within the gentry to recognise that cooperation between them would help to restore order. Disorder continued, however, which laid the foundations for firmer action. Raiding continued over the Border and following the death of Elizabeth I in 1603 there was widespread raiding during the infamous 'ill week'. For ten days borderers pillaged in the West March as far south as Penrith. The motives for these actions are hard to place but insecurity about the loss of an old way of life may have been important. There were also old rivalries between the landed families such as Dacre and Howard but whatever the explanation any remaining goodwill for the clansmen was lost.

After the accession of James I there was a greater recognition that the old lawlessness could not continue and the Union of Crowns made it imperative for the Stuart administration to settle it.

Lord Scrope was replaced by the third earl of Cumberland, George Clifford, who took on the roles of warden of the West and Middle March and was probably more equipped to provide a link between the Border and central government. Clifford was to be the last warden as his ancestor, Robert, Lord Clifford, was the first in 1297. George Clifford also acquired border estates such as Nichol Forest in 1604 and he bid for the Debateable Lands which were finally obtained in 1606 by his brother Francis after George's death. Other land held by the Graham's was also acquired by the Cliffords. The Grahams had continued to be a problem, contributing to border restlessness. In 1605 a contingent of Graham's were shipped to the continent for military service and many soon returned to their homeland as fugitives. A more sustained effort was made to transplant about fifty families to Roscommon in Ireland and a first batch left Workington in 1606. They seem to have been difficult to manage in their new location and were reported to be dissatisfied with land allocated to them. Some returned but may have been less likely to cause further disturbance.

The creation of order on the Border was a slow process, often incomplete and variable according to location. Greater stability was achieved eventually but for a long time the Border area remained as it had been - poor and relatively backward and its infrastructure undeveloped. The later history and final eclipse of the Border occurred in 1603 when it ceased to divide two separate states with the Stuart accession of James VI of Scotland to the English throne as James I. In 1707 the Border ceased to divide two independent kingdoms with the Union treaty.

Chapter 3

The Pilgrimage of Grace, 1536/7

On Market Street, Kirkby Stephen

The turbulent events and religious changes of the 1530's in England in part concerned the eventual rejection of Roman papal authority. The changes were initiated by Henry VIII, a king who held tenaciously to a complete conviction of his own rightness. In effect Henry introduced a religious reformation from a personal need to gain papal approval for divorce from his first wife, Catherine of Aragon. The details of the justifications sought to accomplish this divorce remains a fascinating subject in its own right but will not be pursued here. The culmination of these changes resulted in a popular rising, mainly in the north of England, known collectively as the Pilgrimage of Grace which took place in 1536/7. For Henry VIII the year 1536 has been described as 'The Year of 3 Queens' which again helps to underline an uncompromising attitude and ruthlessness in securing his objectives.

During the various modernisations introduced by Tudor governments the privileges of the Church had been more or less untouched until the arrival of Henry VIII. His father, Henry VII, had consolidated royal power but had left Church privileges alone. The Church probably held one third of all land in England and the income of the great bishoprics and abbeys exceeded that of even the greatest lords. Church courts exercised jurisdiction over ordinary people, often acted corruptly and the Church generally was held in contempt by many. Indeed there was a strong anti- clerical element in the resentment felt by the laity towards the clergy. On the other hand, in terms of belief, the laity were often content with religious orthodoxy and remained suspicious of innovation. The Henrician Reformation was imposed from above by government and the Pilgrimage of Grace was a reaction against the final stages of this process of reform which had set in motion plans for the dissolution of the monasteries.

The complete removal of papal authority from England had been a much longer process and had started with Henry's inability to secure a male heir from his first wife Catherine. It seems that by about 1529 Henry had seriously begun to question the validity of his marriage. Catherine had been married to Henry's brother Arthur and on his death, and in spite of the affinity between them, she was remarried to Henry with papal dispensation.

Henry had also become infatuated with a lady at Court - Anne Boleyn. Papal approval for divorce proved difficult and Thomas Wolsey failed to secure a legal separation from Rome. It was Wolsey's successor, Thomas Cromwell, who planned the eviction of the Pope from England which was accomplished in gradual stages and with considerable respect for legality and statute making. The divorce was finally approved in May 1533 by Archbishop Cranmer following the passing of Cromwell's act in restraint of appeals to Rome of March 1533. In fact Henry had already secretly married Anne Boleyn in January of the same year. The act of Supremacy of 1534 confirmed Henry's Royal Supremacy in the Church and the destruction of papal authority in England. In 1535 Henry became 'Supreme Head of the Church of England'.

Cranmer played a leading role in the English Reformation which commenced as a conservative revolution confirming a victory not of national church over alien domination but a victory of state over church. There was considerable opposition to Henry, particularly in the early stages of these reforms; from the clergy including bishops and many others who remained loyal to Catherine. There were also martyrs including Bishop John Fisher, a long standing Roman

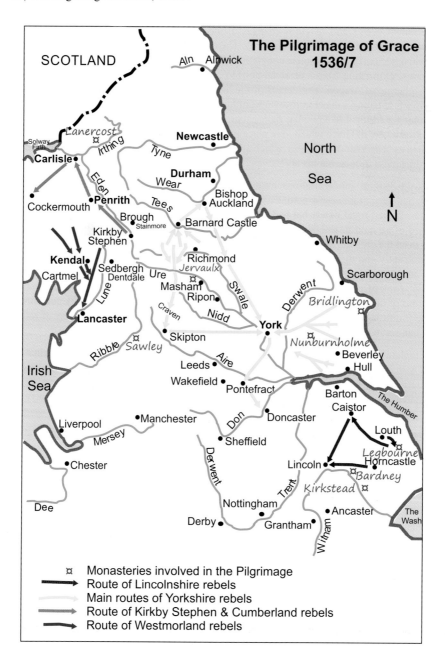

The Pilgrimage of Grace
1536/7

SCOTLAND

North

Sea

Irish
Sea

¤   Monasteries involved in the Pilgrimage
→   Route of Lincolnshire rebels
→   Main routes of Yorkshire rebels
→   Route of Kirkby Stephen & Cumberland rebels
→   Route of Westmorland rebels

The ruin of Lammerside Castle on the west bank of the Eden river. What remains of a fourteenth century pele tower. Peles were small fortresses built in this period for security against raiding parties in the Border regions. The full history of Lammerside is unclear. There are extensive earthworks around the remaining structure. Originally belonging to the Warcop family and at some stage came into the possession of the Whartons and was enclosed within their demesnes probably in the sixteenth century. Wharton Hall is about one mile to the north. A muster of Pilgrims came south to Lammerside from Kirkby Stephen in 1536.

Catholic opponent of Henry, and Sir Thomas More both executed in 1534 for 'malicious denial' of Henry's new title as head of the Church which; *…won the victims immortality and cast a large blood-stain on the new regime.* (J.J. Scarisbrick, Henry VIII).

The rising began in Lincolnshire in October 1536 and coincided with the arrival of the King's Commissioners to dissolve the smaller monasteries. There had been other proposals as well for changes in religious practice and there were rumours that this would involve the closure of parish churches and the appropriation of church goods. As mentioned 1536 was also the 'Year of 3 Queens' in which Catherine of Aragon died, Anne Boleyn fell from favour and was executed and Henry married Jane Seymour.

Few of the leaders of northern society were unaffected by the rebellion either forming sympathy for it or acting under duress to consent to its aims. Sir Thomas Wharton was one of the few whose role in the early stages was equivocal. There were also different strands in the insurrection and some of its aims varied from location to location.

The rising spread rapidly to east Yorkshire and then to Richmondshire and northern England generally including Westmorland and Cumberland. The Yorkshire movement initiated a tax strike in the upper reaches of the dales and letters in the name of Captain Poverty called for a general rising. These letters stimulated risings in the upper Eden valley and Penrith and gatherings spread extensively across Cumberland and Northumberland. Raiding parties were also despatched to these areas to gain publicity and convert additional gentry to the cause. The Richmondshire section seems to have had a more radical anti- landowning element which sought a broader platform of social revolution. The Pilgrimage assumed its final form in Pontefract and its supporters were confronted near Doncaster by an inadequate army assembled for the Crown under the earl of Shrewsbury and the duke of Norfolk. It was the latters aim to negotiate rather than fight the rebels and a truce was reached enabling the opposing forces to disperse with promises of further negotiation over their demands. However, the rebels remained unconvinced and were prepared for war. It soon became apparent that the Crown had lost control of most of the north of England. Some castles remained under royal control including Carlisle, Skipton, Scarborough and Norham. It seems clear that Henry's intention was to yield little or nothing and further negotiations with the rebels by the duke of Norfolk, who remained militarily comromised, probably offered more than the king ultimately intended - including a free universal pardon. The nobles and gentry who had been brought onto the rebels side were directly involved in negotiations with Norfolk and accepted the concessions offered but the commons remained suspicious.

An effigy of Thomas, first Lord Wharton from the Wharton Chapel, Parish Church, Kirkby Stephen. Tough and ruthless he was promoted as a 'new man' by Henry VIII.

In the early stages of the rising there had been local grievances in the upper Eden valley. In October 1536 in Kirkby Stephen it had been the cancellation of the St Luke's Day holiday which sparked off local anger. Later a more comprehensive list of demands was to emerge. One of the central concerns of the Pilgrimage had been the restoration of the monasteries but there were other grievances which, in the case of Westmorland, were more agrarian and economic in content.

On October 15th the vicar of Kirkby Stephen had failed to announce St Luke's Day in three days time since the proclamation of saints days had been forbidden by Cromwell. This loss threatened the autumn livestock fair and the vicar was finally prevailed upon to declare the feast day as usual. A muster had been set at Sandford Moor and it slowly worked its way north to Carlisle having already recruited members of the local gentry into the movement. Robert Pullen and Nicholas Musgrave were chosen for Kirkby Stephen and Christopher Blenkinsop for Brough. A group also travelled south to Wharton Hall and Lammerside in part to persuade Sir Thomas Wharton to join them. The records are not entirely clear whether Wharton spoke to members of the rising, some claim he did. Nevertheless, after this he disappeared or fled only finally reappearing much later at Skipton Castle to join another Crown supporter, Lord Clifford, earl of Cumberland. Wharton's son, Thomas, was sworn into the movement. A further meeting was held at Lammerside to swear in gentlemen to the cause or risk damage to their property.

Two groups then tracked north, on both sides of the Eden, to Penrith to swear in more gentry and commons. A large contingent finally reached Carlisle which was occupied by Sir Thomas Clifford, son of the earl of Cumberland. Further conflict was avoided when a proclamation declared that a truce had been agreed at Pontefract which forbade further assembly. The Pilgrims were finally persuaded to disperse.

It is from this point that some of the more influential members of the rising in the Eden valley ceased to participate. Robert Thomson, vicar of Brough, had been closely involved and it is from him that there is an account of the beginnings of the rising in Kirkby Stephen but he was now to play no further part in the movement. Generally, the clergy were uncommitted whereas the majority of the gentry, under varying degrees of compulsion, had taken the Pilgrim oath with the notable exceptions of Sir Thomas Wharton and the Cliffords. But there were to be other defections.

The truce that had been agreed at Pontefract had been established as a result of the overwhelming rebel army which faced the duke of Norfolk at Doncaster on October 27th 1536. Norfolk had negotiated a truce and free pardon for all rebels but the king thereafter played a skilful and duplicitous game. With hindsight, and bearing in mind the final conclusion to the rising, it is clear that Henry sought fearful retribution. This was accomplished by various strategies; separating gentry and nobility from the commons, provoking breakdowns in the truce, crushing the leaderless commons and, eventually, establishing new methods of governing the north including the border with Scotland.

Further disturbances occurred in Kirkby Stephen in December when Robert Pullen, a member of the minor gentry and one of the leaders of the upper Eden rising, withdrew and was regarded

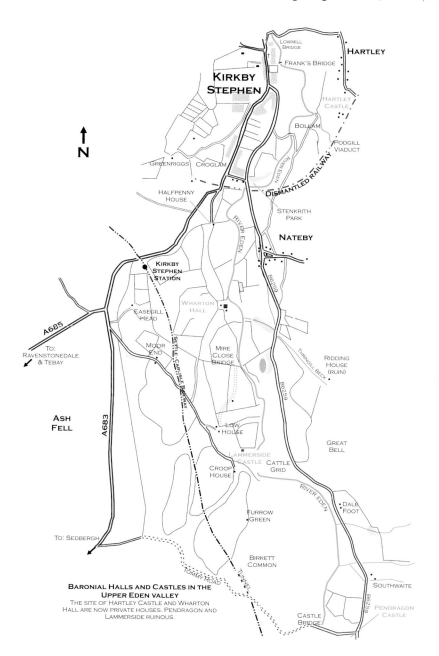

BARONIAL HALLS AND CASTLES IN THE UPPER EDEN VALLEY
The site of Hartley Castle and Wharton Hall are now private houses. Pendragon and Lammerside ruinous.

as betraying the commons. His house was ransacked and he was asked to account for his actions.

In January Thomas Clifford, illegitimate son of the earl of Cumberland, came to Kirkby Stephen in an attempt to capture Thomas Tebay (who had replaced Pullen as a captain of the rising) and Nicholas Musgrave. The two retired to the church tower and could not be removed. There were other disturbances during January and suspicion by the commons that the gentry had betrayed their cause. Robert Aske, one of the principal organisers of the Pilgrimage, had been to London to represent them and had returned with confidence. But further disturbances occurred and serious reprisals followed a rising based on Watton priory. During January Norfolk had received instructions from the king which involved advising lords and gentry that continued support for the commons would result in loss of estates and execution.

Norfolk travelled north via Lincoln, Doncaster and York. He also issued instructions to Thomas Clifford to arrest Tebay and Musgrave at Kirkby Stephen and Clifford arrived with a party of border troopers including some of the notorious Grahams. Again the two retired to the church tower and failure to dislodge them led to the troops taking vengeance on the town and two men were killed. The response from the town drove Clifford and his troops as far as Brougham castle.

The second phase of the Pilgrimage of Grace occurred when 6000 men from the Eden valley and Cockermouth moved north to the outskirts of Carlisle on February 17th. There was an attempt to attack but a party of 500 men from the castle, under Sir Christopher Dacre, drove the rebels south with heavy loss of life and many prisoners taken. This defeat gave the King an opportunity for retribution and on February 19th Norfolk arrived in Carlisle and received his orders to place the region under martial law;

> *...and before you close it up again you must cause such dreadful execution upon a good number of the inhabitants, hanging them in trees, quartering them and setting their heads and quarters in every town, as shall be a fearful warning...*

The commons of the Eden valley were obliged to return to Carlisle on February 20th having lost all. Two former rebel leaders were appointed to prosecute the rebels to prove their loyalty. The Duke of Norfolk was assisted by other loyal gentry; Sir Thomas Curwen, Sir Christopher Dacre and Sir Thomas Wharton.

Seventy four men of Eden valley and Cockermouth were condemned to hang under martial law. Sir Thomas Wharton was present at all the executions in Cumberland and Westmorland and he finally reported to Cromwell:

> *The west borders are quiet*

It has been suggested that the causes of the Pilgrimage of Grace in the Eden valley were in part attributable to the conditions imposed on the population by landowners. Sir Thomas Wharton was one such unpopular and harsh landlord. Neither was Wharton respected for his connections with Thomas Cromwell; first earl of Essex and chief minister to Henry VIII from 1532 until his own execution in 1540 and lord Henry Clifford, earl of Cumberland.

Of the seventy four rebels hanged in Cumberland and Westmorland twenty three came from the parish of Kirkby Stephen and of which nine were from Hanging Lund in Mallerstang. The names are included at the end of the chapter.

The rising in Lincolnshire and the Pilgrimage of Grace was a defeat for the participants and Henry VIII pursued them with careful diligence. The three principal leaders of the rising; Robert Aske, Sir Robert Constable and Lord Darcy travelled to London by their own means under the misconception they would be treated sympathetically. In fact they were imprisoned in the Tower and then faced trial. The former two were returned north for execution at the end of May or early June and Darcy was executed on Tower Hill in London on June 30th. Earlier, in March in Lincolnshire, after the first stage of the rebellion, one hundred men were tried and thirty four executed. Mass executions were avoided in Yorkshire at this time. In the second phase of the rebellion Henry had his sights set on important figures rather than the commons. Afurther twelve significant individuals were questioned, prosecuted and executed along with the three principal leaders. It was a searching and intense settlement which gave Henry a full opportunity to exercise his ruthless imagination.

The result of the Pilgrimage of Grace was that the smaller monasteries were not saved and the rest were soon to disappear very quickly as well. The old catholic faith had been challenged and the justification for it lost. The events of the rising itself are not in dispute although the record is patchy in places but its causes and the catalysts that set it in motion remain the subject of discussion.

There were a variety of reasons for the different social forces to be discontented. The 1530's was a period of change and disturbance and Henry was personally concerned about his succession which came to a crisis in 1536. It is likely that in the country as a whole only a small minority accepted Henry's reforms with enthusiasm. A significant majority probably acquiesced in the changes and a perhaps slightly larger minority were disapproving. All may have been united by a desire to stop the dissolution of the monasteries but beyond this the localised rebellions had different objectives about whether to support the royal Supremacy or return to obedience to Rome.

Northern nobles had the capacity to be disloyal and used their tenants to strengthen their case. Examples here are Thomas Dacre, Thomas Darcy and John Hussey. The gentry had grounds for insecurity as a result of the proposed religious reforms since the monasteries relied on local support to administer their extensive estates. There were factions in Henry's court, some of whom were sympathetic to his first (Catholic) wife Catherine, who may have recognised an opportunity to make a final stand against the King's arrogance. Indeed the instrument of Henry's policy for suppressing the rising, Thomas Howard, the duke of Norfolk, held Catholic beliefs and detested the reforming enthusiasm of Thomas Cromwell. Social and economic grievances were dominant in the north- west and, in particular, in the upper Eden valley where the rising has been regarded by some as having little to do with any aspect of the Reformation. Grievances sprang from the increase in sheep farming and the need to enclose land formerly available as waste. As a result of inflation nobles and landowners had been increasing fines and rents and had become more assertive. Both the Cliffords, earls of Cumberland and Sir Thomas Wharton had reputations for harshness as landlords and the Cliffords, in particular, were significant landowners in Yorkshire and Westmorland.

The consequence of the rebellion for Sir Thomas was his appointment in 1537 as deputy warden of the West March. Henry VIII had also created a new Council of the North based in York charged with the role of overseeing border administration. Henry was keen to reduce the power of the traditional families and gain greater crown control in the north although this was fraught with its own difficulties. The events of 1536/7 created a military crisis because of the strength of support for the rising in the northern counties from all sections of society. The authority and military resources of the noble families posed a threat to the king and many of the gentry, whilst brought back to obedience, were probably not to be trusted too far. The difficulty for the king remained to find a substitute with enough local support to be effective and with enough authority to maintain order.

Wharton's government career went from strength to strength but there was considerable hostility to him and his new authority particularly from the landed families but also from, for example, his tenants over his decision to empark at Ravenstonedale. This latter subject is dealt with in the section on Wharton's deer parks. As mentioned Wharton was quarrelsome and bitter feuds developed with the Cliffords and the Dacres, amongst others, and Wharton complained of a lack of support during his time on the March. During the reign of Mary I the old noble families managed to re-assert themselves and reverse Henry's March policy. Percy in the east and Dacre in the west re-assumed their warden positions although this was to change again under Elizabeth I. In spite of these shifts in royal policy Wharton's career in government service was to run more or less without interruption through four successive reigns and, perhaps, helps to account for the wealth he created in just his own lifetime.

The Pilgrimage of Grace:
Executions in Kirkby Stephen and Mallerstang, 1537

Hanging Lund,	William Shawe, Hugh Dent, Lancelot Shaw, Mallerstang Edward Bowsfell, Richard Wallor, John Bowsfell, Roger Gibson, Jenkyn Wallor, John Rakestrawe.
Hartley	Thomas Hall, William Wallour
Kirkby Stephen	Thomas Tebay, Robert Rowlandson, Edmund Playce, Peter Johnson, Thomas Syll.
Mallerstang	Henry Gibson.
Nateby	Anthony Wharton.
Smardale	Gilbert Denyson.
Soulby	Thomas Wray, Henry Bursy.
Winton	Robert Smythe, Henry Bowsfell.

Sources:

John Breay, *Light in the Dales: Studies in religious dissent and land tenure.* Norwich, 1996.

S.H. Harrison, *The Pilgrimage of Grace in the Lake Counties, 1536-7.* London, 1981.

Chapter 4

The Whartons of Wharton Hall, Kirkby Stephen

Part of 'The Green' Kirkby Stephen

The name Wharton seems to appear first early in the fourteenth century. In 1292 Gilbert de Querton had demonstrated a claim to the manor of Querton. Lammerside castle, a little south of the present Wharton Hall, is claimed to be the first residence of the Whartons before they moved to the present site. Although there is said to be an earlier building slightly to the west of the hall along with the original village of Wharton. The village was moved to Wharton Dykes when the first Lord Wharton moved his tenants outside the pale of his deer park.

The earliest part of the present hall is thought to be fifteenth century, consisting (see plan) of a square three storey pele tower with additional rooms and vaults below.

The Whartons of Wharton Hall, Kirkby Stephen were an old established family who at some stage gained status as members of the minor gentry of Westmorland. The biographical description outlined here is concerned principally with the political and military career of Sir Thomas Wharton (c.1495-1568) although there is also a description of the subsequent fortunes of the dynasty that succeeded him and its eventual eclipse. Additionally there is an outline of the Wharton Mines in Swaledale which more recently have been recognised as an example of both early industrialisation and large scale landscape exploitation.

Sir Thomas Wharton was elevated to the peerage as Lord Wharton in 1544 and achieved prominence partly as a result of changes in the structure of politics in northern England during the reign of Henry VIII and as a result of his personal qualities.

Sir Thomas' career spans the whole of the Tudor age having lived through five reigns and actively served in four: Henry VII, 1485-1509. Henry VIII, 1509-1547. Edward VI, 1547-1553. (Lady Jane Grey, 1553). Mary I, 1553-8. Elizabeth I, 1558-1603.

This continuity and loyalty suggests an astute political actor who managed to avoid royal retribution during both a long career and a turbulent period of history and where even his son spent some time in the Tower of London for his religious belief during the reign of Elizabeth I. The family of Wharton had maintained a history of service to the Cliffords as tenants and dependants. The Whartons held the manors of Wharton and Nateby for the Clifford family, earls of Cumberland, who exercised control over extensive estates in Westmorland and North Yorkshire. Sir Thomas' father had served the crown in the Scottish campaigns of the fifteenth century and had also been involved in estate administration for the northern magnates. Thomas Wharton came to serve in the Percy household, one of the principal noble families of the north, probably by marrying into a family of Percy followers in Yorkshire. In the 1520's Thomas was involved in raids into Scotland under the captain of Berwick along with members of the Percy family. By 1524 he had been appointed JP for Westmorland, an indication of his rising prospects. He was knighted probably in 1527 by Henry VIII at Windsor, returned to Parliament for Appleby in 1529 and was chosen Sheriff of Cumberland 1529-30.

Sir Thomas Wharton's connections with government and members of the Percy family continued until the Percy estates passed to the Crown. Further advancement followed when his authority and income were extended in West Cumberland. The sixth earl of Northumberland had already nominated him to oversee lordships in Catterton and Healaugh in Yorkshire which

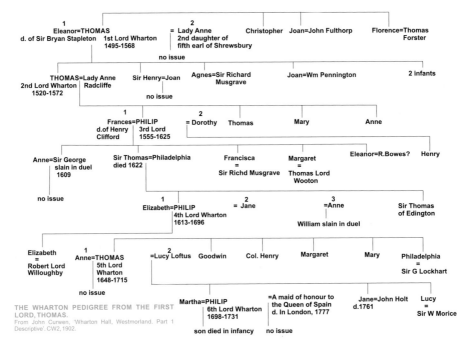

THE WHARTON PEDIGREE FROM THE FIRST LORD, THOMAS.
From John Curwen, 'Wharton Hall, Westmorland. Part 1 Descriptive'. CW2, 1902.

were eventually presented to him in 1536. In 1530 he had been appointed steward of Percy estates in Eskdale and Wasdale, lieutenant of Cockermouth and constable of Egremont castle. These Cumberland posts gave Wharton control of tenants for border service in the West March and were, remarkably, made over to him not only for life but also to his heirs. The accumulation of property and titles indicates that Wharton had gained considerably in stature having shown himself to be a loyal servant to a noble family. The gains seem to have been exceptionally large for someone of his status but later critics were to comment that his estates were acquired piecemeal and were geographically dispersed. Wharton's principal talent was military which he had demonstrated against the Scots with service on the West March. He had also been more closely involved in government service and had, from the early 1530's, been trusted with commissions to the Court by the earl of Northumberland. He was in contact with Wolsey and Cromwell and also the King and was increasingly useful in London.

The events of the Pilgrimage of Grace of 1536/7 were to further strengthen his position. Events in Westmorland just before the rising had also been confused and within the shifting currents of political intrigue it seems that some of the northern gentry including Wharton, whilst feuding amongst themselves, were able to preserve their interests and credibility. There had been considerable discontent amongst the commons as well in Westmorland and Yorkshire. Thomas Clifford had lost the capacity to control his estates and, in spite of his loyalty to the Crown during the Pilgrimage, was one of the reasons why Henry VIII wanted to transfer authority to 'new men' such as Wharton to be responsible for order in the north. Lord Dacre, another major figure in the northern nobility, had already lost credibility with the king and the Percy earls of Northumberland were to fall out of favour during the Pilgrimage of Grace. All this strengthened Wharton's position having remained inactive during the Pilgrimage and later assisting Norfolk in its suppression. In 1537 he was appointed to the position of deputy warden of the West March. The earl of Cumberland remained as Warden although he was to be a figurehead with little real authority. Wharton's appointment was a significant break with tradition and one which did not win support in many quarters. It would have been disturbing for Cumberland that one of his former tenants in Westmorland whose family had earlier served in his household now held a Crown appointment with greater authority than his own. The duke of Norfolk had expressed a preference to Henry VIII for a noble to take the position but he had also argued against either Cumberland or Wharton being involved. It has been suggested that at court Cromwell, another who had also risen by merit rather than inherited title, approved of Wharton's advancement. The political atmosphere had made this a difficult appointment because of the lack of support for Wharton in his own locality. However, Wharton would have been able to rely on the support of his own extended family and he had a reputation for toughness and tenacity in dealing with his enemies. He also had long experience of serving on the Marches, a difficult duty in an often hostile and inhospitable environment and a role which Wharton seemed quite capable of assuming.

In 1542 Sir Thomas was instrumental in leading a small posse of Cumberland Borderers which defeated a considerably larger Scots force in the Debateable Lands near to Solway Moss. In the Battle of Solway Moss the Scots suffered a severe defeat although some argue there was an element of good fortune in the fight. The result was the loss of many lives on the Scots side and several hundred prominent prisoners. Within a week the Scottish King James V, distraught from defeat, had died. For his border service Wharton was elevated to the peerage and made the first Baron in 1544. He also continued to receive grants of land from the crown.

Wharton received a fee for serving on the West March which increased when he became Captain of Carlisle in 1541. His salary doubled when he was made warden of the West March in 1544 following the death of Cumberland and in 1552 he was made deputy warden general of all three marches. This yielded him a substantial revenue and may have equalled his landed income. This income was curtailed briefly after the death of Henry VIII when the new Queen Mary reduced his role only to increase it again when he was appointed as warden of East and Middle Marches in 1555, residing at Alnwick Castle. Wharton also benefited extensively from stewardships of other monastic, church and Crown lands.

Thomas, first Lord Wharton's original inheritance had been the manors of Wharton, Nateby and Shap and from the 1530's he had acquired by gift or purchase the following; a block grant of monastic property including Shap abbey, the manors of Bretherdale (from Byland abbey), Langdale, Ravenstonedale (from Watton priory), Muker and Keld (from Rievaulx), the manor (part) and advowson of Kirkby Stephen (from St. Mary's abbey, York) and the manor of Thrimby, Westmorland. Lands in Appleby, Bolton, Brampton, Great Asby, Long Marton, Reagill, Sleagill and some properties in the barony of Kendal. The manors of Healaugh in Swaledale (from the sequestered estate of Sir Francis Bigod), the two Percy manors of Healaugh and Catterton near Tadcaster and later Healaugh priory and its land. The house and site from Sinningthwaite priory with lands in Yorkshire. Lord Wharton later acquired other manors in North Yorkshire.

After 1557 his warden roles diminished and Lord Wharton finally moved into semi-retirement in 1559 when the earl of Northumberland took over the East March. Later he provided for the foundation of a grammar school in Kirkby Stephen which encouraged a humanist outlook less dependent on the needs of the Church. It probably also acknowledged the greater emphasis on merit and talent by which Wharton had himself advanced. Kirkby Stephen was an early example of other schools that came to be endowed in the region. Wharton supported Robert Holgate's ideals and was perhaps influenced by his example and his career is of some relevance within Wharton's biography. Holgate had started out as a monk in the order of St Gilbert of Sempringham and also achieved, like others in this period, rapid promotion without the support of inherited rank. In 1534 he was made Master of the Gilbertine order and Prior in Watton in 1536. During the Pilgrimage of Grace he too had fled, as Wharton did, in his case to London and after the rising he succeeded the duke of Norfolk and Cuthbert Tunstall as President of the Council of the North to administer the northern region. This was another appointment that was resented by the old nobility. In 1539 Holgate had surrendered Watton and Malton Priory to the Crown and in 1541 was presented with Watton and seven other manors including Ravenstonedale. In 1545 Holgate was appointed Archbishop of York and was to become one of the wealthiest prelates in England.

Holgate had supervised the abolition of the chantries between 1545 and 1547 which adversely affected the operation of schools including those in Brough and Sedbergh. Whilst Holgate was probably an absentee landlord at Ravenstonedale he had made provision for a charitable school in the village and appointed a protestant schoolmaster, Edward Mynese, who had fled from Scotland. Holgate seems to have controlled Ravenstonedale manor from 1536. Wharton finally bought it from the Crown in 1546 and assumed complete control of the manor on the death of Holgate in 1555. Following Wharton's endowment of Kirkby Stephen Grammar School in 1566 Mynese was made its first headmaster. The grammar school was situated in two buildings adjacent to the churchyard in Vicarage Lane.

Thomas first Lord Wharton died in 1568 and is buried at the parish church near to Healaugh priory where he spent his later years. It would seem that there was less reliance on the old ceremonial at the Wharton funeral which was more an occasion for his extended family, friends and neighbours rather than the retinue of an ancient household. His sons were absent including the second Lord Wharton, his heir, for which we have no explanation although it has been suggested that it was a considerable distance from his household at New Hall in Essex. The other main attenders were from within the Tudor administration of Yorkshire and the north of England.

Wharton is interred in the church at Healaugh, near Tadcaster, marked by a marble tomb and there is a sandstone copy in the Wharton Chapel at Kirkby Stephen parish church.

The Hartley or Musgrave Chapel at Kirkby Stephen contains earlier tombs for the Musgraves of Hartley Castle. The Whartons held equal rank with them and it is possible that the Whartons would have wanted to emulate them.

By way of concluding this account of the first Lord it is perhaps worth noting that even quite reliable accounts of him do not hesitate to describe his doubtful temperament, for example John F Curwen in 1902 wrote:

He was a man of fiery temper, and provoked ill-will. It is said he was struck with blindness on Ashfell as a signal punishment. He was in continual danger among the commoners of Westmorland, so he went to reside in the shelter of Healaugh

The Parish Church of St Stephen, Kirkby Stephen today.
'A long, red town church with an impressive Perp(endicular) W(est) tower.' Nikolaus Pevsner, The Buildings of England: Cumberland and Westmorland. (London, 1967).

Thomas, first Lord, Wharton was principally a military man and in social terms belonged to the traditional ruling elite. In spite of the tensions between its individual members he maintained a strong belief in the virtues of order, service and obedience. Politically, he kept faith with these traditional, even medieval, values and continued to serve successive monarchs in spite of disagreements over, for example, the shifts and changes brought about by religious innovation and reaction. By the time of his death Wharton was wealthy and a great landowner, mostly acquired in his own lifetime and from serving the Crown.

When the authority of the traditional nobility came under threat there were new opportunities for men of talent and ambition. Tudor society was not equal but opportunities existed for those offering obedience. Wharton's appointments on the West March from 1537 challenged the widely held belief that those in high office required inherited rank. In moving into service for the government Wharton left behind a world that deferred to the past and tradition. Paradoxically, he remained 'obstinately medieval' in recognising the importance of kinship and the sanction of religion embodied in the old order but he had also worked in the emerging world of a new England and had been rewarded for it.

Like his father, Thomas, second Lord Wharton (1520 - 1572), had a military career in border service, assisted him between 1537-57 and was knighted by Seymour the Protector during the minority of Edward VI after the death of Henry VIII in 1547. Thomas was taken by the rebels during the Pilgrimage of Grace, unlike his father who managed to flee. The second lord was a catholic in religion and he prospered during the reign of Mary receiving both land and authority in the north. Later he became a member of the sovereign's Privy Council and further efforts were made to develop him by being granted a crown property, New Hall at Boreham in Essex.

Under Elizabeth I his religious convictions precluded him from royal favour and he lost influence. In 1561 he was accused of celebrating mass at New Hall, found guilty and was briefly committed to the Tower. Thomas succeeded his father in 1568 and took his place in the House of Lords. In 1569 he was active in the Great Northern Rebellion when the earls of Westmorland

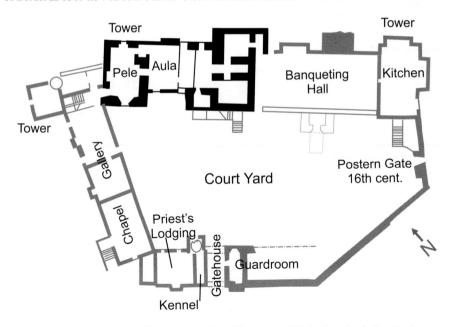

Wharton Hall near Kirkby Stephen. The oldest part of the hall is shaded in black
(after John F. Curwen)

and Northumberland with Catholic support rose to overthrow Elizabeth and establish Mary Queen of Scots on the throne. Henry, second earl of Cumberland and Thomas, second Lord Wharton remained loyal to Elizabeth. Centred at Brougham and Carlisle, Wharton raised forces against the rebels. The effects of the Rebellion were to have a dramatic impact on the northern nobility and the Neville, Percy and Dacre families had their estates confiscated. Only three of the northern nobility remained unscathed; George, third earl of Cumberland still in his minority (the second earl, Henry, had died in 1570), the Scropes of Bolton and Thomas, second Lord Wharton who died in 1572 leaving his son Philip, the third Lord, also in his minority.

The 1569 Rebellion prompted a shake-up of the old order in the north of England. Both the Clifford and Wharton heirs were in their minority at their father's death and were both educated in the south of England during their wardships. Henry Clifford, twelfth Lord and third earl of Cumberland had died in 1570 and his son, George, was placed under the wardship of the earl of Bedford. Similarly, at the death of the second Lord Wharton, in 1572, his heir Philip, the third Lord (1555 - 1625), entered the wardship of the earl of Sussex. Both wardships were, as was usual, overseen by the Crown. The intention had been to try to neutralise the bitter feud between the two families and provide them with a protestant education away from the traditional catholic loyalties of the northern barons. Wardships of this kind were also often used for advantage to facilitate inter-marriage within the nobility. Earl George eventually married Lady Margaret Russell, the younger Bedford daughter. At the same time George's elder sister, Lady Frances, married the third Lord Wharton in 1577. A joint ceremony for both marriages took place in the church of St Mary, Ovaries, now Southwark Cathedral and was attended by Elizabeth I. Earl George was nineteen and lord Wharton, twenty two.

The absence from their northern estates during their minority may have contributed, in different ways, to the disorder that came to afflict their estates. The stability of the Clifford inheritance was slowly dissipated by earl George who eventually concentrated on life at court and embarked on a career as a privateer having become interested in maritime expeditions as a young man. The cost of equipping his naval expeditions and the lack of return on most of his ventures weakened his inheritance in the long term. Few noblemen had enjoyed control of such an inheritance from such an early age.

Lord Wharton also had the opportunity to reside in London in his property at Canon Row. Earl George had also stayed there and they had, in the early 1580's, borrowed money together. Philip was to become involved in re- establishing order on his northern estates including those in Westmorland. In the case of Ravenstonedale, for example, the manor's organisation remained on the basis of its original monastic ownership and had not altered since the time of the first Lord Wharton. Philip negotiated a new agreement with his tenants in 1579/80 and continued in the next few years to reconstruct the powers of the manor court. In general it appears that Philip was not an effective manager. In 1605 his income was £2000 per annum but by 1618 he had debts of £16000.

In 1592 his first wife, Lady Frances, had died at Wharton and Philip remarried to Dame Dorothy Colby. He had settled some of his lands with entail to his elder son George and the rest to his younger son, Thomas. Sir George had married but had no heir and lived a reckless life at court, incurring large debts. He was killed in a duel in 1609 following a dispute over a game of cards. Lord Wharton examined his estate and found he was bankrupt and that all the Westmorland manors were in the hands of creditors. Philip's second son, Sir Thomas, undertook to take over his brother's debts in conjunction with his father and recover the titles of the manors including the core holdings of Kirkby Stephen, Nateby, Wharton and Ravenstonedale. The fines levied on tenants were also renegotiated

Ravenstonedale had been excluded from this provision because of the previous agreement reached with Lord Wharton in 1579/80. The effects of these agreements and the efforts of the king, James I, to abolish tenant-right had been to limit the harsher conditions imposed on tenants by their landlords and to give greater security. One of the reasons for Lord Wharton entertaining the king at Wharton in 1617, apparently at great expense, was in the hope of receiving lenient treatment over tenant rents and fines. Hence the mounting debts of 1618 which obliged Philip, third Lord, to put his financial affairs in the hands of trustees. Philip died in 1625.

The second and third lords made less mark than the first. It is said that the third lord sat in the House of Lords for forty years without ever addressing the house. A more generous assessment has been made of Philip, fourth Lord Wharton (1613 - 1696):

> *In him the fortunes of his house were restored, while his bible charity represented that moderate Puritanism which has remained the dominant culture of the dales.* *

The fourth lord, Philip, was the eldest son of Sir Thomas and Lady Philadelphia Wharton and he was born not at Wharton but at Aske Hall near Richmond. Sir Thomas and his wife were both devout Puritans who passed on their religion to their sons. Sir Thomas died in 1622 predeceasing his own father, the third lord, who died in 1625. Philip thus acquired the barony as fourth lord from his grandfather. The family estates had been in the control of a relative appointed to rescue the old lord's affairs from disorder and debt. It was to be a further ten years before Philip came fully to his estate.

* John Breay, Light in the Dales. 1996. p.70

The inheritance was, however, substantial including the dispersed northern properties and, eventually, through his second wife, he also acquired large estates at Winchendon and Wooburn in Buckinghamshire. There were also lead mines in Swaledale in Yorkshire which brought income and is discussed in more detail at the end of the chapter.

Two nicknames are associated with Philip. During the Civil War he served on the parliamentary side. Wharton had been appointed Lord Lieutenant of Buckinghamshire in 1642 and led a regiment at the battle at Edgehill. His regiment and others fled the field and for a time he hid in a sawpit. He was later to be taunted by Prince Rupert as Saw-Pit Wharton and the name stayed with him for the rest of his life.

It seems he had not acquired the military skills of his family and he avoided further action by immersion in parliamentary matters. Politically, he supported moderation and disapproved of the execution of the king. He also supported the restoration of Charles II. In religion he supported dissent and provided protection in Ravenstonedale for dissenting clergy. Christopher Jackson had been ejected from his parish at Crosby Garrett and found a new position there. It has been noted that both a Presbyterian chapel and a Quaker Meeting were established in the parish during his lifetime.

The second nickname associated with Philip is the Good Lord Wharton because of the charitable distribution of bibles among poor children in counties associated with his family - Westmorland, Cumberland, Yorkshire and Buckinghamshire which continues to this day.

The fourth lord died in 1696 in London and he was buried at Wooburn. He was husband to three wives, two of them wealthy, and father of fifteen children, of whom six died in infancy. It has been said that his reputation for good works did not extend to his children who found him a stern parent. Principle mattered more than friendship and he supported neither king nor politician if they worked against his own belief.

The fifth Lord Wharton, 'Honest Tom'(1648 - 1715) succeeded to the title at his father's death in 1696. He inherited a substantial estate and is reputed to have spent vast sums on electioneering and horse racing. He had already married a great heiress in 1673 who died in 1685 and he married again, to Lucy Loftus, in 1692 who brought him another £5000 per annum. Thomas entered parliament in 1679, a champion of liberty; he is credited with the formation of the Whig party. (Whig refers to a political party opposed to the Tories. The term was first used in Charles II reign and soon referred to those placing William III on the throne, displacing James II.)

In 1688 Tom Wharton drew up the invitation to Prince William of Orange to come to England. William appointed Wharton as controller of the household and a privy councillor. In 1706 he progressed in the ranks of the peerage to Viscount Winchendon and earl of Wharton. In 1708 he was made Lord Lieutenant of Ireland to serve 1709-10. In 1715 George I created him baron of Trim, earl of Rathfarnham, marquis of Catherlough (Carlow) in the Irish peerage and marquis of Wharton and Malmesbury in Great Britain. He died in the same year.

The final and tragic chapter of the Wharton dynasty lies with Philip, sixth lord Wharton (1698-1731). In 1715, at the age of seventeen, he:

> '...succeeded his father in all his titles and abilities, but none of his virtues.' *

Philip's baptism had been sponsored by William III but by the age of sixteen he had already married secretly which may, it has been suggested, have been the cause of his father's death. This brought him early to his titles and a large income.

In 1716 he went to Geneva to be tutored in Calvinism and was created duke of Wharton in 1718. In politics he shifted from being a Whig to a Tory and became president of a free thinking Hell Fire Club. Later he adopted the Jacobite cause in support of the restoration of the Stuart monarchy and became a Roman Catholic. By 1725 he had left England never to return and in 1726 the Pretender 'James III' made him duke of Northumberland.

He was wilful and reckless in expenditure and lost a large sum in the South Sea scheme. He was outlawed by the House of Lords ostensibly for serving as a volunteer in the Spanish army. His first wife had died in 1726 in London and he married again to a lady serving in the Spanish court.

In 1721 the young duke had been unable to cover his debts and he passed all his Westmorland estates to trustees to be sold. They were administered until 1729 and then sold to Robert Lowther of Maulds Meaburn of the family of the earls of Lonsdale. The sixth Lord Wharton continued a reckless life and died in 1731 at the age of thirty two in Spain. Philip's sister, Jane, survived him and died in 1761, the Wharton title becoming, to all intents and purposes, extinct.

All the estates became privately owned except that portion in Yorkshire used for charity to provide the Wharton bible. In 1844 a colonel, Charles Kemeys Kemeys Tynte, claimed the barony of Wharton and obtained a reversal of the sixth lord's outlawry. In the process four other descendants of the fourth lord were shown to have an equal right to the title and the claim did not proceed.

* Edward Ross Wharton, The Whartons of Wharton Hall. 1898, p. 52

Wharton Hall fell into decay following its purchase by the Lowthers. The main block of the Old Hall is probably fourteenth century or early fifteenth century. Most of the later addition was made by the first lord Wharton and reflected his improved status. A new Great Hall with kitchen was added in about 1540 and a gatehouse and north west range around 1559. The original Old Hall was restored by the first Lord Lonsdale around 1785 along with the north west range. The later hall and gatehouse remained ruinous.

'Wharton Hall, Westmoreland'
from *Philip, Duke of Wharton 1698-1731* by John Robert Robinson, (London, 1896).

As a postscript to this outline of the Wharton family an account of the Swaledale lead mines would be useful in view of their proximity to the original Westmorland and Cumberland estates. By the seventeenth century the Wharton family had consolidated substantial estates in upper Swaledale. The first acquisitions were made by Thomas, first Lord Wharton at the time of the dissolution of the monasteries and under the patronage of Henry VIII. Muker was so acquired in 1544 and part of Healaugh manor in 1556. Whilst in the early years the family were absent from Swaledale the later Whartons were to make a substantial contribution to mining development in the county as a combined result, it would seem, of accident, business acumen and a profitable connection with local agents.

Philip, fourth Lord Wharton, inherited his title, at the age of twelve, in 1625. Philip lived with his family at Aske Hall, Richmond. Philip's father Sir Thomas Wharton had predeceased his own father (Philip, third Lord Wharton) and hence the title passed to Philip the grandson. As the fourth Lord Wharton Philip took a strong interest in his Swaledale estates completing, for example, the purchase of the remainder of Healaugh manor in 1635. This new acquisition included some small estates with coal and lead mines and these were continued by him. Philip's second marriage brought him a dowry of two manors in Buckinghamshire, Wooburn and Winchendon, and they settled there permanently in 1658. Philip, the fourth Lord, continued an active political and military career at a national level. In order to develop his mining interests in Swaledale he drew on the local expertise of the Swales family who had worked for the Whartons at Aske Hall. Robert Swale managed their Swaledale estates for forty years and this continued with his son, Philip, when Robert Swale died in 1662. Philip Wharton had been instrumental in supporting religious nonconformity continuing the earlier Puritan commitment of his parents. The Swales' were first generation Quakers and Philip Wharton took an active part in establishing Quaker meetings in the dale. A partnership developed between Wharton, Swales and a mining engineer, Robert Barker. Wharton retained his controlling interest but it seems clear that a sound working relationship developed over the long term bringing prosperity and stimulating further exploration. At the time of the handover of the Wharton agency from Robert to Philip Swales in 1661 the Friarfold, Merryfield and Lownathwaite mines were very active. Many new trials were initiated later in the seventeenth century and the new mines were able to benefit from existing smelt mills including those owned by Wharton. It is worth mention that the period of greatest mining activity occurred in the following century and after Wharton control lapsed. Earlier sites such as Beldi Hill mines behind Crackpot Hall were extended in the eighteenth century and continued to work as late as the 1880's.

Philip, fourth Lord Wharton, died in 1696 and was succeeded by Thomas, fifth Lord (1648 - 1715). The fifth Lord became a prominent member of the Whig party encouraging the accession of William of Orange to the English throne. Thomas gained additional titles as first Earl of Wharton and, in 1715, Marquess. An immensely wealthy man Thomas was able to invest large sums for electioneering purposes. Land disputes over mining rights in Swaledale were not uncommon partly due to an absence of "free mining" rights and the domination of access to land by the Crown or powerful landowners. One complex and prolonged case involved control of the Grinton mines which started in 1696. The village of Grinton is located south of Reeth and the river Swale. Just west on the north side of the river was the Wharton manor of Healaugh. Reginald Marriott (a deputy auditor in the Exchequer) claimed a right granted by the Crown to mine for lead at Whitaside and Harkerside in the parish of Grinton. The claim was challenged by a local landowner, Sir Solomon Swale, who claimed he owned a separate manor of "West Grinton" separate from Grinton. The Court ruled against Sir Solomon and he then made another attempt to regain these mines in 1705. In 1706 Thomas, fifth Lord Wharton, claimed Harkerside and Grinton Moor belonged to his manor of Healaugh. Wharton seems to have been concerned to limit Marriott extending his mining operations in the area and began to sink new mines adjacent to those already in operation by Marriott. The intervention by Wharton may have related to the value of lead brought out by Marriott a few years earlier. Marriott gained an injunction restraining further encroachments by Wharton and filed a lawsuit against him. The subsequent trial became a celebrated case involving over three hundred witness statements. As both parties were either landowner or employer neither were in a position to provide evidence from unbiased witness depositions in view of their economic dependence. In 1708 the Court decided against Wharton on the grounds that the river Swale provided a clear terrotorial boundary excluding claims to ownership of land south of it. It may be recalled that the manor of Healaugh lay north of the river. The separate claim by Sir Solomon Swale against Marriott was heard after the Wharton case and again the claim was defeated. Further legal attempts by Swale to gain redress were unsuccessful and Swale died a ruined man after spending time in prison for debt.

The upper reaches of Swaledale

Thomas Wharton's unstable son, Philip, sixth Lord, succeeded to his title as Marquess of Wharton in 1715 and through extravagance quickly fell into debt. In 1721 his estates had been forfeited to the Crown from whence trustees settled his debts. The remaining income passed to his two sisters and finally to a niece, Anna Draycott, who married George Fermor, second Lord Pomfret in 1764. The manors of Healaugh and Muker had been sold separately leaving the mines and mining rights with the trustees and beneficiaries. Eventually the mines went to the Denys family and continued to be worked vigorously. The London (Quaker) Lead Company with extensive mining interests in North Wales, Derbyshire and Alston Moor became involved in mining in Swaledale taking a lease on part of the Wharton Gunnerside Mines and after 1745 introduced improved methods of mining and smelting which contributed to the continued exploitation of the dale.

The Blakethwaite mines at the northern extremity of Gunnerside Gill were constructed and developed by the successors to the Wharton mines.

Top: *Blakethwaite smelt mill started in 1821. Fuelled by two ore-hearths using local peat and small amounts of coal. Fumes were drawn into a flue and ran up to a now demolished chimney on the crag above.*

Below: *Blakethwaite peat store used peat cut from moorland above and was stored in this open-sided building.*

Chapter 5

The Wharton & Ravenstonedale Deer Parks

*Ravenstonedale looking north (c. 1872) from
The History & Traditions of Ravenstonedale, Westmorland
Vol 2 by Rev.W.Nicholls.*

It may be useful, when discussing the deer parks and deer walls created by Thomas, first Lord Wharton, to place them in a wider context. It has been said that deer parks were a visible statement of individual power and influence and on this basis the parks created by Lord Wharton fit well into this frame. Park owners practiced social exclusion by removing tenants to the outside of a perimeter boundary and they expressed their ambition by re-arranging the landscape to suit their own needs and preferences. These factors were not peculiar to Lord Wharton but occurred throughout England and across an extensive time frame.

Even royalty had to consider the effects of their plans. Edward IV had to compensate townsfolk when he expanded Windsor Park in 1467. In 1482 he expanded Castle Donington in Leicestershire and gave up 402 acres of his demesne to persuade tenants to give up common rights to land he wanted to build on. Cornbury Park in Oxfordshire was created from a hunting lodge in the royal forest of Wychwood and was disafforested in 1642. Parks were sometimes resented and laying waste to a park was a form of protest. By 1400 the peasant population was also placing pressure on land to expand into. In much of England by 1450 the park began to be seen as an amenity rather than an economic resource.

It can also be shown that the form of parks altered and evolved as they adapted to changes in circumstance. There were particular conditions, which will be discussed shortly, within the economy and culture of medieval Cumbria which also played a part in the evolution of the deer park in the region.

Parks have ancient origins and evidence shows that over three thousand years ago enclosures were used to contain animals and livestock. In India aesthetics and wisdom were combined and celebrated in the park. Today, many public parks are a focus for leisure and recreation. It has been usual to suggest that the medieval park was introduced to England by the Normans but it is now thought likely that the Anglo-Saxons did also use parks. They consisted of enclosures to retain stock, either animals of the chase or domestic livestock. The zenith of the medieval park probably lay in the period 1200-1350 when its contents were used as a ready food supply for households. They were an integral part of the medieval economy providing not only meat but many aspects of the needs of subsistence including fuel, building materials, winter feed and bedding.

At first parks were designated by the crown and baronial lords who managed them under the manorial system and their use would have been controlled and regulated for the rest of the community. There were also other forms of regulation particularly for hunting in areas designated as 'forest' and governed by 'forest law'. A park was one of four recognised hunting grounds; forest, chase, park and warren. Each was closely regulated and in the case of parks permission was required for their creation. In fact the latter three forms of hunting were available to private individuals and were exempt from forest law but chases were normally only available to those of the highest social position.

In a sense the park became more popular for private individuals because royal forests became too restrictive and hunting, between 1200-1650, became more ritualised providing an opportunity to display courage and endurance. Of course, it remained exclusive because it required land ownership as a precondition. In the Tudor period park making therefore increased but sometimes at the expense of the peasantry who found their hamlets and burial grounds behind the park pale. It was also a period when there was greater social stability although the effect of border strife in the north did have a negative impact. Developments elsewhere, for example in architecture, reflected a cultural shift from the defensive to the domestic, and from castle or fortified structure to mansion and palace. By the eighteenth century park and house came together as an integrated scheme eventually to be conjoined by garden design. The dissolution of the monasteries had assisted the availability of land. Between 1540 and his death Henry VIII sold, gifted away or exchanged two thirds of monastic land among about one thousand people. Many monastic lands already had parks and provided opportunities for obtaining land in remote locations. A park became an ingredient in the recipes of success.

The northern perimeter of Ravenstonedale Park deer wall.

With regard to Cumbria the two deer parks that form the starting point for this chapter, at Wharton and Ravenstonedale, can be described as late examples of the medieval manorial park. Within the context of deer parks this type of park accounts for the great majority but they are also the most difficult to document because records of them are scarce. The density of parks in Cumbria is also less than in lowland England. There are estimated to have been over fifty manorial parks in Cumbria and, of course, many have disappeared as part of the ongoing process of enclosure and agricultural improvement.

But there are clues about them from old maps when, for example, field or house names refer to previous usage as 'park' which is carried over in the name. In the vicinity of Wharton there is evidence of earlier parks at Brough, Ewbank, Tebay (Roundthwaite) and Wet Sleddale amongst others. There is also a clearly defined perimeter of a park at Crosby Gill, Crosby Ravensworth where old enclosed pasture adjoins heather moorland on the limestone upland and where traces of a high wall remain. Closer to Kirkby Stephen there are faint traces of old park enclosures at Hartley Castle divided into Park Hill and Castle Park. On nineteenth century maps Wharton Hall was subdivided into four parks; Low, Nateby, New and High Park (see illustration). Above Pendragon Castle in Mallerstang there is an enclosure described as 'The Friths'. 'Frith' is an old word thought to refer to a park-like enclosure connected with game preservation within the old hunting forests. Apart from changes in land use which affected parks one factor which influenced their retention into the modern period was continued residence in the area. Many owners from amongst the nobility and gentry became absentees, ceasing to live in the area and leasing their land for farming.

The more notable examples of deer parks came from the larger parks created as part of a baronial estate. These parks either adjoined a baronial castle, as at Cockermouth, Kendal, Millom and Greystoke, or were located nearby as, for example, at Appleby where the park was situated at Flakebridge a few miles away. There were also forest parks which were either crown property as royal forest or controlled by baronial lords as private chase. Examples of private chase would have been the forests of Mallerstang and Stainmore both controlled by the barons of Westmorland. Parks were a feature in these vast domains such as the royal forest of Inglewood to the south of Carlisle and the baronial forest of Whinfell associated with Brougham Castle. The use of upland forest for hunting declined in the face of stock grazing and occupation by an expanding peasant population. Most of the baronial castle parks had been dismantled by the seventeenth century.

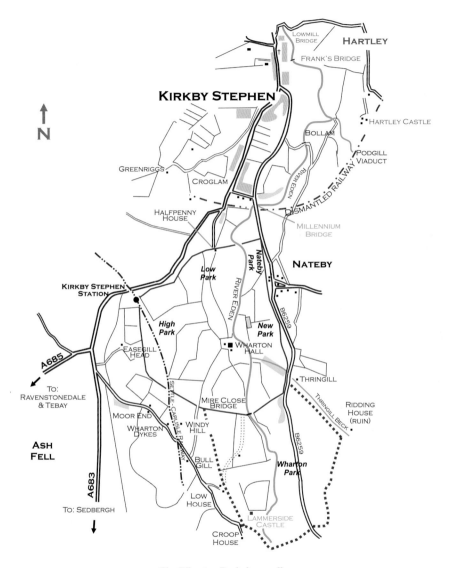

The Wharton Park deer wall

The creation of the original park in the sixteenth century obliged tenants to be moved outside its perimeter to Wharton Dykes. The most likely outline favours a circular park (red line) but an alternative suggests an extension (dotted red) to include Lammerside Castle. Later the 1862 six inch Ordnance Survey sheet divided the circular park into four (High, Low, Nateby and New Park) with Wharton Park occupying the extension.

Based on the 1;25000 OS Sheet First Series NY70 1950/1

Deer parks were created by the first Lord Wharton in the sixteenth century at Ravenstonedale and Wharton just to the south of Kirkby Stephen. The Wharton park deer wall has been dated at 1547 and its boundaries have been established from a map of Wharton estate dated 1638. Originally, the park boundary was thought to be identical with the whole estate embracing the tower at Lammerside and the lower fell side east of the Eden and north to Thringill. It is now believed that the park itself was more circular in shape with Wharton Hall at the centre and additional ground south and east being Wharton demesnes. In this frame Mire Close bridge would have been the southern limit of the park and, moving east, it would have run on the west side of the B6259 Nateby road. The foregoing has been documented in an article by R.W.Hoyle, 'Thomas Lord Wharton's parks at Ravenstonedale and Wharton' (CW 2, 1995) where further evidence for the park is also put forward because of a dispute between Wharton and the young earl of Cumberland in 1554. The earl had objected to the obstruction of his right of access to free chase in the forest of Mallerstang as a result of the construction of Wharton's deer wall.

The original Wharton deer wall at its best can be seen as it traverses north, just west of Nateby village and parallel with the road before turning sharply west to cross the Eden. On this section the wall remains on private land and can only be viewed either from the road or where rights of way intersect with it - for example where the public bridleway enters Wharton land just on the northern edge of Nateby village. The best state of preservation was from Halfpenny House (grid; 769071) to Kirkby Stephen railway station where a few remaining sections reached the original height and limestone slabs laid horizontally at the wall top were still visible (photograph). Since 2011 much of this section has been rebuilt. The Ravenstonedale park wall is located north of the village and its northern perimeter lies on the parish boundary. It is here that the wall is seen to its best advantage reaching to three metres in places. It can be approached either on access land from Smardale bridge or on the public bridleway which leaves the A685 Ash Fell road (grid; 736047) moving north where it briefly joins the edge of the park wall. The park is roughly oval in shape. Both parks suggest they were quite capable of containing livestock including deer. It is thought that Wharton park did contain deer whereas Ravenstonedale may have been used for grazing cattle.

The Ravenstonedale wall was constructed using tenant labour in 1560-1 shortly after Lord Wharton came into full ownership of the manor. In 1877 the Rev Nicholls collected some details about its construction including the irony of the 'love boons' demanded by Wharton. The boons required the original tenant occupiers of the enclosed land be responsible for the labour in constructing the wall in proportion to the land they possessed. The walling was paid for either in cash or credited against tenant fines. The tenants were compensated with parcels of land outside the pale of the park. It seems that sixty nine tenants, some with very small land holdings, were involved in this surrender and allocation of new land. The tenants at Wharton were also obliged to surrender land in exchange for land at Wharton Dykes outside the park perimeter. It is thought that both parks were commercial ventures and would have involved major alterations to the landscape.

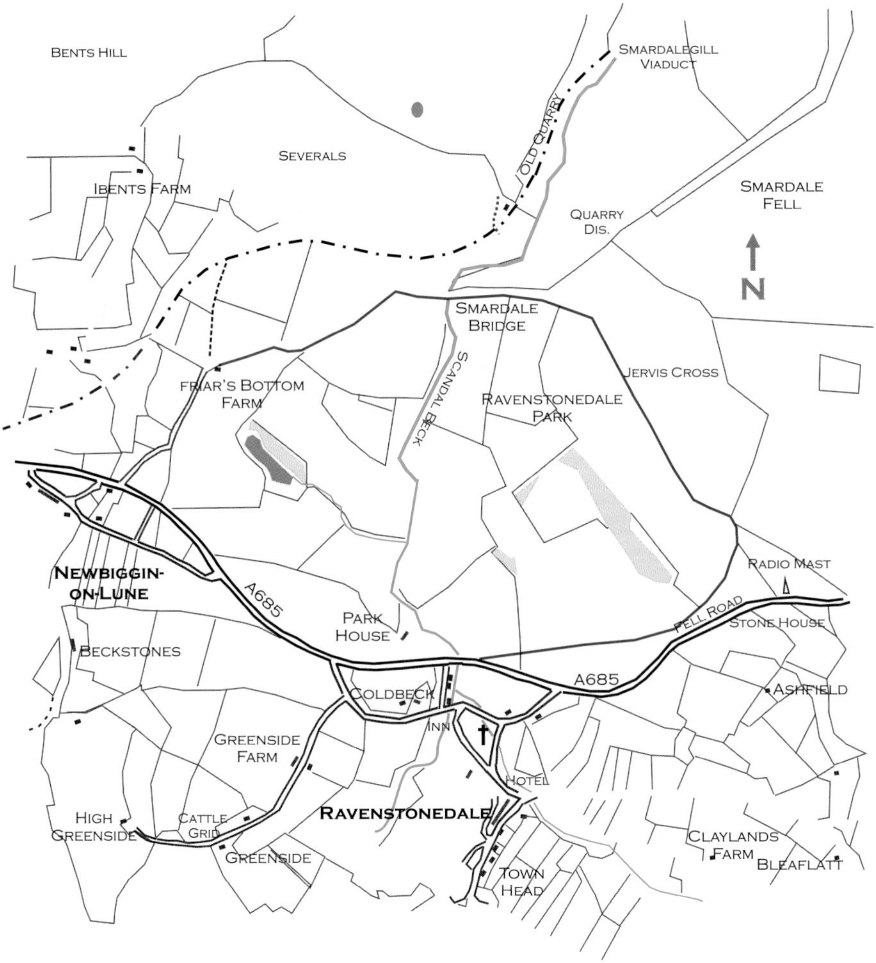

BENTS HILL

SEVERALS

SMARDALEGILL
VIADUCT

IBENTS FARM

OLD QUARRY

QUARRY
DIS.

SMARDALE
FELL

N

SMARDALE
BRIDGE

SCANDAL BECK

JERVIS CROSS

FRIAR'S BOTTOM
FARM

RAVENSTONEDALE
PARK

NEWBIGGIN-
ON-LUNE

A685

PARK
HOUSE

RADIO MAST

FELL ROAD

STONE HOUSE

BECKSTONES

GOLDBECK

A685

ASHFIELD

GREENSIDE
FARM

INN

HOTEL

HIGH
GREENSIDE

CATTLE
GRID

RAVENSTONEDALE

CLAYLANDS
FARM

BLEAFLATT

GREENSIDE

TOWN
HEAD

The Ravenstonedale Park Deer Wall

The line of part of the park wall is marked in red where it is still visible on the ground.

Based on the 1:25000 OS Sheet First Series NY70, 1950/1

*The Wharton deer wall with topstones below Kirkby Stephen (Settle-Carlisle) railway station.
This original section of the wall was replaced with a new wall in 2011 when a new footpath
from Halfpenny House to the station was constructed.*

Chapter 6

Kirkby Stephen Town & River:
Mills & Manufacture

Former barn on Faraday Road, Kirkby Stephen.

This chapter will examine in detail aspects of the mills and manufactures within the Kirkby Stephen economy. In particular the role of the river Eden in providing water- power for its mills and as a focus for transport communication. The chapter will start, however, with a discussion of another facet of the domestic economy; namely the production of hand-knitted stockings which has a long history in the wider area although much of it has been difficult to document in detail*. The historical focus remains broadly based, however, since in many instances information about this aspect of the town is limited by an absence of detailed records. This is mitigated somewhat by drawing on other sources that provide comparable experience from within the locality. The intention is to provide a thematic survey of what is known by drawing on existing historical and literary sources rather than exclusively archival research which can be both time consuming and unproductive. What is immediately striking is the localised nature of water-powered mills which of course confirms a feature of pre-industrial economy across Britain. It also underlines that by the early modern period control of the Kirkby Stephen economy and its hinterland was divided across three manorial courts; Clifford (later Hothfield), Musgrave and Wharton (later Lowther). Each manor would have created separate sources of control and power about how local resources, including water, were utilised and exploited. Lords obliged their tenants to take corn to the manorial mill for grinding and heavy fines were imposed for going elsewhere. Often the tenantry were expected to keep the mill race in good repair and the miller invariably took a portion of grain for his services. In medieval times the mill was an important resource and efforts were made to prevent Scots invaders gaining control over them.

Historically the rural economy of Upper Eden was based on agriculture supported by other part-employments. One small component of part-employment was mining; in this area normally for coal and lead and details of this have been described in the chapters on the Upper Eden Upland. In Kirkby Stephen town there were of course many other craftsmen; carpenters, masons, slaters, tailors, shoemakers, saddlers, millers etc.. It was a subsistence economy and an important component of part-employment was the production of knitted stockings by men, women and children which went largely unrecorded as domestic and family work. The production of hand-knitted stockings was undertaken mainly by the poor and attracted subsistence wages. It was also seasonal and taken up in the winter months when agricultural work was least available. Changes in the nature of a local economy like Upper Eden emerged only slowly and can be said to commence in the sixteenth century as local trades and crafts developed, accelerating later in the next century. In some cases, and particularly in textiles, improved techniques of processing emerged much earlier and, in the case of fulling, were introduced as a precursor of industrial processes applied later across the whole textile sector in fibre preparation, spinning and weaving. The early development of fulling as a process will be returned to later in this chapter. Here it need only be said that fulling is an ancient process going back as far as Roman times. The process involves removing superfluous grease and oil from cloth by pounding it to mat together loose fibres to shrink and felt them. Originally this was achieved by trampling or

---

* Please note that at the end of the present chapter there is a referenced list of books and articles. The content of the chapter is detailed and the author considered that it may be useful for some readers to be aware of how its conclusions have been reached and the sources used. On the other hand these references may be ignored, if preferred, as they do not alter the main themes discussed.

walking woollen cloth in water and urine with some added ingredients but by the twelfth century the process was mechanised by water power using wooden mallets. Fulling as a process formed a significant part of textile activity in the northern dales and Lake counties. Early weaving and fulling mills formed an important part of a wider economy extending to major centres such as Kendal. It is evident that there was a degree of cross-fertilisation between all these sectors of textile activity and not just in Britain but extending into Europe as well. Indeed it is difficult to fully identify where such developments first surfaced. Daniel Defoe's (c.1660 - 1731) account of knitted stocking production in Richmond in North Yorkshire was published in 1724:

Here you begin to find a manufacture on foot again, and, as before, all was cloathing, and all the people clothiers, here you see all the people, great and small, a knitting; and at Richmond you have a market for woollen or yarn stockings, which they make very coarse and ordinary, and they are sold accordingly;... This trade extends itself into Westmoreland, or rather comes from Westmoreland, extending itself hither, for at Kendal, Kirkby Stephen, and such other places in this county as border upon Yorkshire; the chief manufacture of yarn stockings is carried on; it is indeed a very considerable manufacture in it self, and of late mightily encreased too, as all the manufactures of England indeed are[1].

It is perhaps worth mentioning that whilst Defoe became a prolific writer and journalist he started out in business as a general merchant dealing in hosiery, woollen goods and wine.

It was two centuries earlier and after the Dissolution of the Monasteries (1536 - 1541) that the acquisition of monastic property enabled the lesser gentry to become actively involved in the process of wealth creation[2] and one useful example of this has been described in Chapter 4 with the Wharton family. It is difficult, however, to generalise about the growth of population and prosperity before 1800 because statistics are incomplete and factors operating against economic well-being in medieval times included border violence, foreign war and disease.

These were all factors which contributed to the unpredictable nature of economic life in medieval times and the conditions for hardship and poverty. However, it has been estimated that in Westmorland an increase in population began in the reign of Elizabeth I (1558 - 1603) although it remained small in comparison to neighbouring Cumberland and northern England[3]. Hitherto, as noted in a survey of probate inventories, much of Cumbria bore the hallmarks of a *subsistence economy* characterised by standardised possessions, low levels of geographical and social mobility and minor differentiations in wealth amongst the bulk of the population[4]. In general land ownership in Cumbria tended to be more evenly spread than other parts of England. It has been estimated that in the mid-eighteenth century one third of land in Cumbria was in the hands of customary tenants although there were also some large estates with significant landholdings. In many respects this formed a basis for tenants working the land to resist change and to reinforce a pattern of family subsistence[5]. In addition major landowners in the area around Kirkby Stephen were, in many cases, semi- or non - resident[6].

A combination of subsistence agriculture, customary tenants resisting change (or having to accept low levels of prosperity through subsistence) and a degree of aristocratic absenteeism probably contributed to a degree of neglect and a lack of other opportunities. The escape from *poverty, unemployment and distress* is largely born out by the outflow from the region through emigration in the nineteenth century when this became a viable option. It was not just the unemployed who migrated but those who feared unemployment or an uncertain future and the outflow from a largely rural district such as the Upper Eden Valley was significant[7]. By way of example the population of the northern region of England (including Cheshire, Derbyshire, Nottinghamshire and Lincolnshire to the border with Scotland) more than doubled between 1851 and 1911 as a result of industrial expansion whereas the population of rural Westmorland expanded by only 9%[8]. This reflects not only the significance of out-migration to other parts of Britain or abroad but also the difficulty of attracting new employment possibilities into the area. The continued reliance on low paid domestic work such as knitting and spinning in marginal areas such as the Upper Eden Valley is in part explained by the absence of other employment opportunities within the locality.

An expansion of the wider economy did however make an impact, albeit slowly, on a more traditional and hierarchical way of life. A case in point are the domestic textile industries of the area of which the neighbouring town of Kendal was a major centre. Amongst other trades in Kendal this involved spinning, knitting and weaving on a large scale along with associated activities such as scouring, bleaching, fulling, dyeing, and additional finishing processes. (By way of comparison in 1801 the population of Kirkby Stephen parish was 2515 and Kendal 6892). The historical development of many of these industries have generally been documented but what has been called the *North Pennine knitting industry* has left few traces[9]. Earnings were small and the work required little equipment. As a result whilst many writers through time have referred in passing to stocking knitting in the northern Dales including Kirkby Stephen there is in fact little detail about individual knitters or where the additional processes such as yarn spinning, dyeing, fulling and finishing were carried out.

The situation is clearer for Kendal than it is for Kirkby Stephen as will be discussed shortly. The Westmorland census of 1787, although incomplete and unfortunately with no return for Kirkby Stephen, lists over a third of females as knitters in the parish of Stainmore[10]. More recent writing on the subject has emphasised that hand knitters earned low wages and that knitting was undertaken by the poorest classes in country areas where there were few alternative work options. From later in the seventeenth century knitting was seen as a way of keeping the poor employed and thereby not being a charge on the poor rate[11]. It was an employment that could be taught from an early age and was amusingly described by the Lake Poet Robert Southey in; *A true story of the terrible knitters e'Dent* published in 1834. Using Westmorland dialect the story relates a tale of two young girls who run away from a knitting school that drove them very hard to learn to knit; *an' then we o'knit t'hard as we cud drive, striving whilk cud knit t'hardest yan again anudder*[12].

It is worth emphasising that it was the development of domestic, locally based trades, such as knitting and spinning in an earlier subsistence economy, which finally emerged to cater for a wider, national market. A corollary of this is that the location of, for example, the textile industries shifted as a result of technical innovation and specialisation. It is why we can record at a simple level how the knitting industry finally moved away geographically from rural areas such as Westmorland as a result of the introduction of forms of mechanical reproduction in other parts of Britain. This happened slowly but in the early modern period was stimulated by government policy, for example in the final years of Henry VIII's reign, when there was an attempt to limit imported goods and encourage technical innovation. Changes in fashion had also eventually influenced the contribution knitted stockings made to the national economy. Although until recently a neglected subject it has been estimated that by the early seventeenth century every household required two pairs of stockings and were more likely to buy ready made than produce their own[13]. In addition there was a significant export market and a need to supply hose for military use both at home and abroad. However, even earlier in the 1590's, stocking knitting was an *immense industry, employing men and women knitters* (Thirsk) and this was before the mechanised stocking frame industry got properly going[14]. Knitting was also geographically dispersed taking place in Wales, Cornwall, some Midland counties and Durham, Yorkshire, Cumberland and Westmorland.

Amodern work on knitting first published in 1951 as *The Old Hand-Knitters of the Dales* has become an important benchmark for literature about the hand knitting industry of the northern Pennine dales[15]. The work highlights many of the early and important sources of information on the subject and is particularly useful for understanding the extent of hand knitting activity in the old county of Westmorland and the Yorkshire Dales. In Westmorland apart from Kendal and Kirkby Stephen it flourished in many other villages including Crosby Garrett, Mallerstang, Orton and Ravenstonedale. As mentioned important new research has emerged since this time but the outline provided by Hartley and Ingilby remains important. It has already been noted that few traces of the part-time occupations of either knitting or spinning remain. Neither made an impact on local records and the identity of individual knitters (and spinners) remains mostly a mystery[16] but it is now acknowledged that hand knitting was an occupation pursued by men, women and children, although in the sixteenth century may have been done mostly by women and children according to some accounts. However, the employment of men for hand knitting was a feature in the Dales in the nineteenth century where this occupation probably persisted for the longest time[17]. One historian of Cumbria has noted that whilst probate references relating to knitting are rare there was an entry for Robert Dickson of Nateby (a village adjacent to Kirkby Stephen) for 1678 for; *stockings woollen and yarn, £7*[18].

The literary and historical references relating to knitted stockings in Westmorland remain interesting and in the main relate to the account originally outlined by Hartley and Ingilby. Following Defoe's observations published in 1724 an article in Gentleman's Magazine in 1754 reported on Kirkby Stephen as follows:

The whole village consists of one single street, indifferently built...There was once a fine market place, 70 yards wide, and near 100 yards long, but by some strange inattention to public utility houses have been suffered to be built on it...The market is on Monday, and as the stocking manufacture supplies the principal trade, this traffic is the first at the market; it generally begins about six, and is over about eight in the morning. Though the situation of Kirkby Stephen is under bleak and barren mountains, yet the communication with several of their own dales, and with Yorkshire, along the river heads, affords a pretty considerable market, an advantage which Brough, near Stanemore, has now lost for want of such connection[19].

A drawing by Thomas Fawcett is reproduced here from the Hartley and Ingilby volume which depicts the stocking market in Kirkby Stephen as it was perceived to be in the nineteenth century[20]. The location is on Market Street in front of what is now Croft House. Another useful and early source of information about this trade came from Arthur Young's *A six months tour through the north of England* published in 1770[21]. It provides a comprehensive description of the extent of the Kendal textile trade and its importance in the broader Westmorland context. It is probable that as machine power began to have a serious impact on the more domestically based industries in the nineteenth century the knitted stocking trade persisted but finally began to die out towards the end of the century. Of course changes in fashion had also taken place with the decline in use of long hosiery. By the early eighteenth century cotton had also begun to replace wool and linen as a material for clothing.

The Stocking Market, Kirkby Stephen, 1817.   *Thomas Fawcett.*
(*By permission of Miss M. Mason*).

The Stocking Market, Kirkby Stephen, 1817
From Marie Hartley and Joan Ingilby, The Old Hand-Knitters of the Dales (1951).

Readers may be interested to note that this drawing by Thomas Fawcett (see Chapter 7) is not included in his Sketchbook although there is one very similar of Croft House without the figures on the right. The figures are knitters offering their products at the market.

In Penrith Arthur Young describes: *the employment of the women and children spinning, and some knitting*. But Kendal is identified as the centre for several *manufactories the chief of which is knit stockings*. The trade divided into several branches in wool combing, spinning and knitting. In addition Young identified further employment in making Kendal cottons and linsey woolsey, both woven fabrics using different qualities of coarse regional wool. The yarn was spun by local farmers and brought to market every week for weaving. It can be suggested that whilst towns such as Kirkby Stephen finally came to specialise in hand knitting the business of spinning and also weaving did occupy the town to some small degree but finally much of this trade became concentrated in Kendal with middlemen taking on the task of distributing spun yarn into the wider area and then collecting knitted stockings as an end product.

Later in the nineteenth century other local writers and historians referred to knitting more as an activity receding into the past. Rev. Nicholls in writing of Mallerstang indicated that *knitting was a universal occupation where men as well as women engaged in knitting, with which they occupied themselves as they were walking along the road, or in interval when they were shepherding. Their work when done they took to James Law, of Outhgill, (in Mallerstang) forty years ago. He kept a draper and grocer's shop......and took the knitted work to Kendal, or sent it by the carrier*[22]. From Kendal the final destination was to dealers in London. We learn about the importance of this connection with London from the discovery of the business records of Abraham Dent (1729 - 1803), an eighteenth-century Kirkby Stephen shopkeeper[23]. In one respect these records provide a glimpse into the business activities of one man in a remote northern market town towards the end of the century. But Dent's activities are portrayed as untypical because of the diverse range of business activities he engaged in; groceries, stationery and sundry goods and later he became a hosier, brewer and wine merchant. It is significant that after these records were found (in an attic in upper Wensleydale after over one hundred years) they yielded useful insights into an otherwise obscure area of study with little documentary evidence. However the author, T S Willan, repeatedly acknowledges the absence of any testimony from Abraham Dent himself about what appears to be one of his most important trades - that of hosiery and knitting. But Willan's book about Abraham Dent is important because its subject concerns one Kirkby Stephen tradesman and sheds light on an aspect of Kirkby Stephen life which was previously

Old Shambles, Market Street, Kirkby Stephen c. 1895.

An old spinning gallery which was a feature of seventeenth and eighteenth century farmhouses. There were others at Ravenstonedale, Newbiggin-on-Lune and Adamthwaite. The only access to the first floor was often an outside staircase.

Drawing by Jane Tilley

undocumented. Yet the book is also significant because it raises other questions to which there are still no answers and its author was quite honest in identifying these limitations.

Because information about the knitting trade is limited the reasons Willan uses to arrive at his conclusions about Abraham Dent in his capacity as hosier and knitter will be described. In addition it provides the opportunity to assess some possible historical contexts within which Dent might have operated. First of all Willan distinguishes between a shop trade that Dent conducted (which received goods from one hundred and ninety suppliers between 1756 - 1777 from across the country including many varieties of woven cloth) and, on the other hand, the knitted stocking trade. Willan later remarks that apart from Dent's surviving business records nothing else indicates that he was involved in stockings and that there is little information about how this knitting industry was organised; *It seems clear that two types of people were engaged in it, the hosiers and the knitters, but both remain elusive. Abraham Dent was never described as hosier, though he was one*[24]. A little earlier Willan had also remarked that; *the origin and development of the industry remain obscure*[25]. But he does speculate that one explanation could be that a buoyant and extensive woollen woven cloth trade in Westmorland had declined dramatically by the late sixteenth century as a direct result of changes in government policy. An article which outlines these earlier changes in the woollen trade in northern England is used to question whether the adoption of hand-knitted stockings as a trade was made as a response to an economic recession in the region which impacted, by the sixteenth century, on *northern sheep farmers, spinners, weavers and fullers*[26]. The same period was one of expansion in the woollen trade in other parts of the country. In medieval times the monasteries had developed a wool trade in the north and, it is argued, a great majority of the coarse wool clip was sold outside the locality including export to the Low Countries. Kendal did however develop as a coarse woollen centre by the end of the fifteenth century. Edward VI had been instrumental in encouraging home manufacture and Tudor legislation prohibited raw wool export. One consequence was to enable manufacturers in other parts of the country to monopolise the wool trade and to use better quality wools available outside the remote northern counties. Probably Kendal survived as a woollen centre because it was flexible and already had an established reputation with a woven cloth output based on coarse artisan cloths (Kendal Green). To what extent these changes impacted on the remoter dales of Westmorland is unclear but there has been a recognition that they were negatively affected by changes in national policy and also the Dissolution: *The fulling mills in the fell valleys, however, gradually disappeared or were put to other uses....and increased poverty added to the many existing social problems of the north*[27].

Returning to Abraham Dent and the question of the organisation of his knitting business Willan notes that his wool was not purchased locally but came from County Durham or Newcastle and concludes that Dent *bought wool and sold stockings*[28] but also admits that no records survive for us to answer this questionin more detail[29]. The difficulty lies in estimating how the raw wool was converted into stockings because this would have required various intermediate processes; sorting and carding (and possibly combing) wool, spinning into yarn, knitting, dyeing, washing (or scouring or fulling), stretching (tentering) and pressing. However, further consideration and the testimony of earlier commentators such as Daniel Defoe and Arthur Young disposes

Willan to conclude that Dent's stockings were probably woollen (not combed worsted yarn which were produced in Kendal) and normally undyed[30]. Whilst not dyed it appears that they were washed on account of soap supplied in quantity to John Cleasby who may have acted as Dent's agent in Swaledale. Abraham Dent was trading as a hosier on a significant scale in the period 1760 - 1780 although it is estimated by one important local antiquarian that the trade originated in the previous century[31]. There must have been a significant amount of knitting carried on which was probably not recorded because it was part-time work and, of course, there are no figures for Kirkby Stephen from the first Westmorland census of 1787. According to Willan two contemporaries of Dent appear to have been engaged in acting as hosiers in the town: John Barnett who died 1782 and on a lesser scale Thomas Fawcett. The latter appears in Dent's accounts as a supplier in 1769[32]. Perhaps a more significant figure antecedent to these contemporaries was John Thompson (1633 - 1721) who Willan cites as a hosier wealthy enough to leave generous bequests to benefit local people[33]. In addition Thompson is thought to have developed a prosperous hosiery business with a fulling mill at Stenkrith and possibly a dyehouse in Kirkby Stephen. However, there seems to be few traces of this business continuing after his death. Stenkrith Mill is dealt with in the section on water-powered mills and seems to have been put to various uses although information about its origins and history are also limited. However, it is worth considering whether there were any connections between Stenkrith Mill and the local hosiery trade. Abraham Dent continued in hosiery into the later 1770's supplying military contractors. The trade was effected by carrier to Kendal and then onward to London. Much of his trade went to the American colonies but his sales declined noticeably with more settled conditions across the Atlantic during the 1780's. Dent had also noticed that it had been more difficult to secure the cooperation of local knitters but the reasons for this are also unclear. Abraham Dent operated in a national market which would have been susceptible to various external forces such as changes in fashion, market demand and technical innovation but how these effected him is not known. It would seem that Dent experienced some financial inconveniences later in his career, but he had also remarried, moving to live in Wensleydale having retired from shopkeeping but continuing in a small way as a hosier *until at least 1789*. He died in 1803. His younger son Abraham may have helped his father in hosiery but eventually it appears he worked with his elder brother as a brewer.

From the manufacture of knitted stockings we can move on to the series of water powered mills which were based on the Eden river in and around Kirkby Stephen. Some attention will be given to map the means by which the power of the river was utilised before continuing to explore in more detail aspects of textile processing that was conducted at some of these mills. However, it should be stressed that some of this is necessarily speculative because of the limited information we possess about the early domestic economy of the town. Starting north of the town is New Bridge. Its location would suggest that it was an ancient crossing point. Prior to the Tebay to Brough road the pack horse route passed through Gaisgill, Raisgill Hall, Kelleth and Brownber (north of Ravenstonedale) before crossing Smardale Bridge for Waitby. At Sandwath Bridge the route joined Green Sike Lane (see map, now a public bridleway) to cross the Soulby road and join the river Eden which was crossed, according to John F. Curwen about 150 yards below New Bridge: *there is still a deep track up* (from the river) *just beyond Eden Mount*[34].

*New Bridge: The road layout today
with public bridleways*

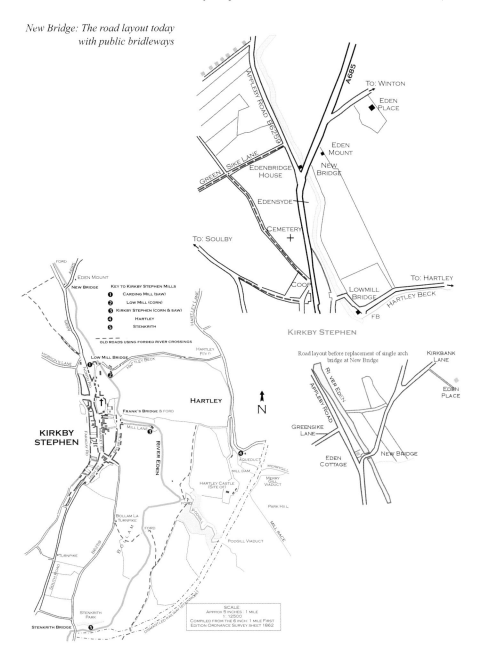

KEY TO KIRKBY STEPHEN MILLS

❶ CARDING MILL (SAW)
❷ LOW MILL (CORN)
❸ KIRKBY STEPHEN (CORN & SAW)
❹ HARTLEY
❺ STENKRITH

OLD ROADS USING FORDED RIVER CROSSINGS

Road layout before replacement of single arch
bridge at New Bridge

SCALE
APPROX 5 INCHES : 1 MILE
1 : 12500
COMPILED FROM THE 6 INCH : 1 MILE FIRST
EDITION ORDNANCE SURVEY SHEET 1862

The first edition 6 inch to one mile OS map confirms the track although Eden Mount was not in existence in 1862.The origin of these local bridges is often obscure and so easily taken for granted that their alteration often went unrecorded. In Anglo-Saxon times the advantages of trade and peace had been established and by Domesday royal authority had underpinned the need for road and bridge maintenance. This process would have been prolonged in the Kirkby Stephen area because of Border disputes. The Domesday survey did not include Westmorland because the county had not been brought fully under English control.

Whilst great monastic bridges were created in the medieval period the exact dating of the main bridges in and around Kirkby Stephen is difficult. Local conditions also played their part. It is thought smaller stone arched bridges in the district only began to appear after the Restoration of 1660 and particularly after 1760 when turnpike traffic increased. Curwen tells us that by 1744 - 5 reference to a *stone bridge* at New Bridge suggests that its structure was still unusual[35]. Prior to this timber gangways were more frequently used to cross rivers. Invariably records state bridges are *seventeenth century* (for example) which is the case when identifying at what stage a particular structure began to be made in stone. Prior to this such bridges were more primitive. On pack horse routes rivers were either crossed at fords, stock bridges (wooden planks supported on logs or, later, rough stone piers) or narrow single arch structures that could later be widened with additional supports. The modern New Bridge seen today was created in the 1960's.

The next bridge moving upriver is Low Mill, a seventeenth century double arch stone bridge spanning the Eden and providing access to Hartley village. It was listed as Grade 2 in 1957. The 1862 six inch OS sheet indicates that the first mill adjacent to the bridge was a carding mill before its later use as a saw mill after about 1860. Originally water powered using a sluice from the weir upstream. The weir disappeared in the winter of 1962 - 3 after a heavy flood. In their book *Kirkby Stephen*[36] the authors note that it was built as a textile mill for carding wool by Richard Farrowday (Faraday) and Thomas Haistwell (Hastwell) about 1799 although another source suggests there was a cotton mill on the site built (or rebuilt) in 1787[37]. Water also powered the flour mill on the Hartley side, known as Low Mill. Perhaps so named because of the

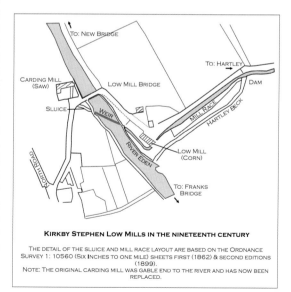

KIRKBY STEPHEN LOW MILLS IN THE NINETEENTH CENTURY

THE DETAIL OF THE SLUICE AND MILL RACE LAYOUT ARE BASED ON THE ORDNANCE SURVEY 1: 10560 (SIX INCHES TO ONE MILE) SHEETS FIRST (1862) & SECOND EDITIONS (1899).
NOTE: THE ORIGINAL CARDING MILL WAS GABLE END TO THE RIVER AND HAS NOW BEEN REPLACED.

Low Mill weir from a postcard c. 1900.
Looking south from the bridge with Low Mill on the left hand bank.

Above: *Lowmill race on the Hartley Road with St. Stephen's church in the background. circa 1910*

Left: *Dam and sluice above the former Low Mill.*

existence of Hartley High Mill in Hartley village. The dam adjacent to the Hartley road is still in place and the remains of the mill race which ran parallel to the road down to the mill is still visible. Low Mill would be the earlier mill owned by the Musgraves of Hartley Castle. It is thought to have been operating in the fourteenth century and was repaired by the Musgraves in 1754. Joseph Clark is noted to have occupied the mill in the mid nineteenth century as the miller. The mill was still operating after World War Two and was finally converted for residential use in 1974.

It may be useful at this point to return to the carding mill at Low Mill bridge and mention two aspects of broader relevance to it; firstly to the Faraday connection with this mill and secondly the subject of textile manufacture that was ostensibly carried on both at these mill premises and within the locality of Kirkby Stephen. The processing included carding and wool spinning (at the carding mill) and fulling at Stenkrith Mill. The extensive domestic manufacture of hand knitted wool stockings has already been discussed earlier in this chapter. There have been other textile manufactures originating in Kirkby Stephen, for example with blankets, silk fabrics and hats, but establishing details about these additional trades remains ongoing. There was also a cotton mill for a brief period circa 1800. The foregoing will be expanded on in the sections that follow.

The name Faraday has cropped up already (Chapter 9) where it was noted that a stream on Hartley Fell, close to Nine Standards, is named Faraday Gill and also a ruined stone building adjacent is named Faraday House on early OS maps. There is also a quarry close to Faraday Gill which may have a connection with the Richard Faraday under discussion here. Faraday House has been variously referred to as a *shieling* (a seasonal shelter in an upland area), a refuge for quarrymen working in the vicinity and as a shooting hut. These suggestions probably all contain a grain of truth but, as with other interpretations, caution is required in drawing firm conclusions. There is also no exact correlation with the identity of the Faraday used to so name these features in the landscape but there is a strong indication that it was the Richard Faraday who at one time owned the carding mill. It is worth mentioning, however, that whilst we have clear references to the carding mill at various stages in its history there remains no continuous history of the mill or its origins.

One of the reasons for the knowledge we do have about the Faraday's of Kirkby Stephen is due to the *father of electricity* Michael Faraday (1791 - 1867) - who contributed immensely to scientific developments in the nineteenth century in the fields of electromagnetism and electrochemistry. During the eighteenth century the Faraday family had become established at Clapham Wood Hall near Settle in West Yorkshire. Robert Faraday and Elizabeth Dean had married in 1756, farmed a 46 acre smallholding and managed a water driven weaving mill. Robert also earned income as a slater. They produced ten children. One of these, Richard Faraday (1757 - 1815), moved to Kirkby Stephen for reasons unknown although limited resources for an expanding rural family in the eighteenth century meant that migration was not unusual. Richard married Mary Hastwell in Kirkby Stephen in 1777 and worshipped at the Sandemanian chapel in what is now Arcade Royal to the rear of Market Street. Mary's grandfather had tenanted Black Scarr Farm in the parish of Kaber at one time - a farm no longer in existence but thought

RUINED SMITHY, OUTHGILL
James Faraday, father of Michael, worked and courted his bride at this hamlet.

The image is taken from The Hammer and the Anvil: A background to Michael Faraday by James F. Riley (Clapham, 1954)

to be close to the site of the former Belah Viaduct and near to Oakbank[38]. By the time of Richard Faraday's death in 1815 he had become a successful man of business owning two houses and at least one mill. The mill was for carding and spinning wool although an earlier connection with cotton spinning has also been suggested. Richard Faraday's will confirms his main business as wool spinning and it seems that this business continued to specialise in blanket manufacture until its conversion to a sawmill. James Faraday, a younger brother to Richard, followed his brother to Westmorland and worked as a blacksmith at Outhgill in Mallerstang.

James married Margaret, sister to Mary Hastwell, in 1786 (working as a maidservant at Deepgill Farm (across the Eden river from The Thrang). Two children were born to James and Margaret at Mallerstang (Elizabeth and Robert) before moving to what was the edge of London at Newington Butts, Southwark. It was here that Michael Faraday was born. From his humble family origins in Yorkshire and Westmorland Michael Faraday was largely self-educated and seems to have chosen to pursue a career as a scientist when there were few obvious paths for someone with limited resources. Some fortunate circumstances propelled Faraday to become a laboratory assistant at the newly established Royal Institution where initially he had to cope with a difficult relationship with Humphrey Davy. Throughout his celebrated career he maintained a strong faith in his Sandemanian religion and whilst seeming to conflict with a scientific view of the world it would appear to have assisted him in revealing what he saw as the grand design of the universe.

It is probable that Richard Faraday gained occupational experience from his family in Yorkshire with both a water powered weaving mill and in slating. At his death his will specified his family members as beneficiaries to his estate and from a large family (and at least four children who predeceased him) this included his wife and children John, Hannah, Jane, Richard and James. The eldest son Robert's entitlement was contingent upon the settlement of an existing debt of £34 to one Andrew Craig.

Richard Faraday's Will confirmed him as the owner of a carding mill and as a wool spinner also owning *the close or enclosure of land called Mill Close adjoining the mill dam*[39]. A *Faraday Genealogy* produced by later family descendants noted his occupations as grocer and slater[40]. He may also have been incorrectly described as an innkeeper. There is a record of an alehouse keeper's recognizance (a surety normally registered with a local magistrate) of 1806 between Robert Faraday, innkeeper, and Richard Faraday, cotton spinner[41]. The reference to *Richard Faraday cotton spinner* remains intriguing in view of the brief existence, about this time, of a cotton mill in Kirkby Stephen called the factory or manufactory[42]. This will be returned to again shortly. A few years later either a son, or grandson (of Robert Faraday), called Richard is noted to have become landlord of one of the sixteen Kirkby Stephen inns, the White Lion, in 1825 according to a local newspaper[43]. By the time of the Kirkby Stephen Tithe Map of 1842 Mill Garth, adjoining the weir, remained in the possession of John Faraday as both owner and occupier whereas Low Mill Carding Mill was owned by John Addison[44]. The stone double arched footbridge (also Grade II listed) over the river on the edge of the main town is known as *Frank's Bridge* possibly after Francis Birkbeck who established a brewery adjacent to the river in the nineteenth century. The bridge is located at the foot of a narrow walled lane called *Stoneshot*. It is another ancient crossing point and ford.

Frank's Bridge from a postcard circa 1920.

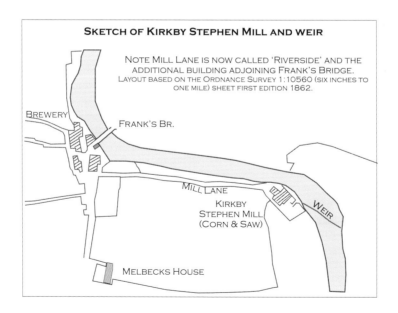

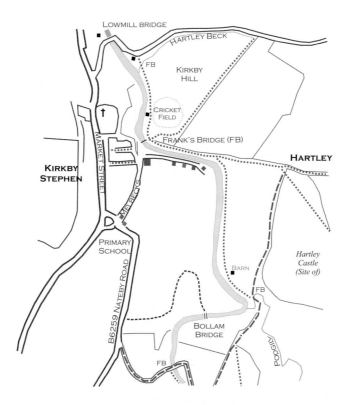

Frank's Bridge and surrounding area

On the west bank of the Eden above Frank's Bridge was another water-power mill known as Kirkby Stephen High Mill or Riverside and also with an occupier's name. In this case at the time of the 1842 Tithe Survey it was owned by the Earl of Thanet and occupied by Joseph Blacklin. This mill probably was the early manorial mill for Kirkby Stephen located close to the original manor house in Melbecks. It was used for corn milling and as a sawmill and was water-powered by a weir which has again been destroyed in the process of time. The Blacklins occupied the mill for over eighty years. At this stage we can journey into the centre of town to the site of a former cotton mill which only had a brief existence at the beginning of the nineteenth century. At this time there would have been a strong motive to invest in many of the new opportunities that emerged in the textile industry. One company that became established in Kirkby Stephen was one producing hats operated by a Mr Titley[45]. Possible motives for investment in cotton spinning would have been stimulated by the success in the previous century of two pioneering figures of invention and industrial organisation namely Jedediah Strutt and Richard Arkwright[46].

Strutt was to invent a machine to produce ribbed knitted stockings (instead of knitting by hand). To exploit the potential of cotton as a new yarn source for hosiery Strutt partnered with Arkwright to create the first cotton spinning factories, a process which began in 1769. Strutt was based in Derbyshire and Arkwright moved from Lancashire to Nottingham to develop the revolutionary idea of applying water-power to machinery within the factory system. In the Midlands three major hosiery industries were based on cotton, silk and worsted (wool) and there clearly was a market for cotton hosiery[47]. In any event over the following decades it became a major stimulus for many other people to seek their fortune in the same manner. It spread as far as the Pennine dales although few were to be successful in their chosen field but many did manage to adapt and create niche markets within the context of Empire trade. It is remarkable that both Kirkby Stephen and Brough had their own cotton mills probably based on hand operated machines and it is perhaps not a surprise that the fortunes of the Kirkby Stephen mill did not last long being only remotely connected to major centres of trade. The Manufactory or Factory as the cotton mill became known was a substantial building located to the north of the Parish Church in an area known as The Green.

The former Union Cotton Mill and later workhouse, Kirkby Stephen. Photograph by Mike Davies-Shiel. Reproduced with the permission of Cumbria Industrial History Society.

The building was demolished in the 1960's and replaced by an apartment block. There are a number of conveyance documents recording changes of ownership in the period 1747 - 1810 in what starts as being described as a tenement *part of which became the factory*[48]. The description for these transactions seems to suggest that changes were occurring to this tenement and other premises that resulted in ownership passing to someone capable of erecting a new building. Unfortunately the records are not entirely clear[49]. In 1773 a conveyance surrendered possession to Thomas Pearson junior (from his father) who is *admitted to the premises that now constitute the factory*. In 1791 ownership passed to William Crawford and two years later to Thomas Perceval. In 1795 it passed to Joseph Dent and in 1802 to his nephew John Dent and then in 1803 to George Dickinson. Other sources suggest that a rebuilding occurred after this time. According to Parkinson's Guide (1922) by 1807 the bankruptcy had occurred of Graves, Lane & Co who had established a cotton mill on the premises. In any event it seems likely that this company name could be incorrect and could be noted as Degraves, Lane & Co., managed by Peter Degraves who had *issues of debt, bankruptcy and falsehood* attached to his name through most of his life[50]. In 1807 the building passed to a banker called John Dand who attempted to continue the business and who in turn became bankrupt in 1809. At this point The Manufactory is described as *lately rebuilt and new modelled* and an agreement made for its sale to Richard Binks including looms and *frames for dressing cotton warps* at Stenkrith Mill[51]. It is not known what happened to the business but the building was finally leased to The Visitor & Guardians of the Poor of Kirkby Stephen to become the East Ward Workhouse in 1818.

The remaining mills were Hartley High Mill and Stenkrith Mill and now both demolished. The former was a small corn mill located on the east bank of Hartley Beck below the site of Hartley Castle. It was abandoned when the Stainmore (Durham & South Lancashire Union) railway was completed in 1861. Traces of the mill dam remain but much of the headrace was overlaid by Merrygill Viaduct. However, a mill race is marked on the first edition OS six inch scale map originating below Ewbank Scar and the runoff under the railway viaduct is still in place (see map: *Key to Kirkby Stephen Mills*).

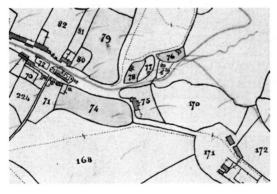

A section of the Hartley Tithe Map 1839 drawn by W. Powson illustrating the position of Hartley High Mill. Each field plot and/or property is identified by number. Note the lane adjacent to Plot 71 is the modern footpath to Kirkby Stephen. Plot 75 and property lies adjacent to the road to the site of Hartley Castle at 171/172. Hartley High Mill is Plot 229 between Plots 76 and 77 and consisting of two small buildings. Cumbria Archive Centre, Kendal. WDRC/8/135.

PLOT	TITLE	OCCUPIER
229	Mill	Thomas Chapelhow
74	Harker Croft	Robert Hamilton
76	Hartley Cottage	Robert Hamilton
77	Mill Garth	Thomas Chapelhow
78	Cottages	William Hebson

Most traces of Stenkrith Mill are gone although the site can still be identified along with the mill race, the path of which is still visible around the perimeter of what is now Stenkrith Park. A culvert with a stone lintel issues into the river Eden adjacent to the mill site but is no longer in use. This may have been an early fulling mill later adapted for corn. In fact two buildings occupy the site at Stenkrith and detail about the operation of the smaller of the two buildings is limited. The introduction of fulling mills occurred prior to the mechanisation of other textile processes in carding, spinning and weaving. Fulling involved two separate innovations which in combination dramatically reduced labour content to a supervisory role. These were the adoption of water power and the use of hammers to pound woven fabrics to shrink, felt and stabilise them. What seems likely is that the use of fulling mills extended rapidly during the thirteenth and early fourteenth centuries and particularly in rural areas such as the Lake District[52]. The adoption of a manorial mill was, like the corn mill, an investment opportunity for profit since it could be made a monopoly to which tenants would be obliged to subscribe. However, the benefits of fulling in remote and rural areas did not only benefit the lord of the manor but also those able to work outside the restrictions imposed by urban guilds. Whilst little evidence is available about the early operation of Stenkrith Mill it can be recognised that potentially some of these early conditions were met as they were on a large scale in Kendal and district[53].

The now demolished corn mill at Coldbeck, Ravenstonedale circa 1900.

The particular geology at Stenkrith also provided the conditions for a steady flow of water outside the main course of the river Eden as it plunged over a faultline known as Coopkarnal

Hole. The main fall of river water would have been difficult to utilise directly for water power because of massive fluctuations in water volume during flood periods from the upper Eden catchment. However, a collapsed cave system adjacent to the main waterfall consisting of rock fissures and gorges provides a slow and constant flow of water. The Tithe Map for Stenkrith does not do full justice to the amount of water that could have passed through this area above the mill to provide its water supply. Traces of the mill race are still visible and the Tithe Map also locates an adjacent tenterfield (Tenter Close) a south facing hill slope suitable for drying and stretching finished cloth. More work is needed to establish how early the mill came into existence, the type of fabric produced and the degree of mechanisation of the fulling process. Local records indicate that a Kirkby Stephen hosier John Thompson (1633 - 1721) occupied Stenkrith Mill for fulling. At the time of the Tithe Map (published 1842) the owner was Charles Alderson and occupier Thomas Race. In 1834 Christopher Blades was in occupation and according to a trade directory an earlier occupier, in 1829, was John Oversby. Like Hartley High Mill, Stenkrith was eclipsed both by the Stainmore railway and the general transition from water to steam power. The railway itself needed land for its own trackbed but eventually facilitated the transport of textile and milled products from further afield rendering local, small-scale supply uncompetitive.

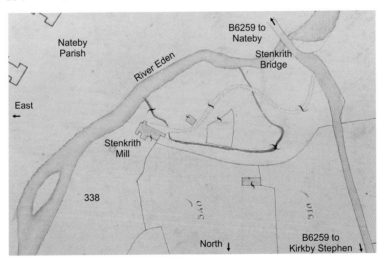

A section from Kirkby Stephen Tithe Map (drawn 1839) depicting the location of Stenkrith Mill. Cumbria Archive Service, Kendal. WDRC/8/169

PLOT	TITLE	OWNER	OCCUPIER
338	Backside Pasture	Charles Alderson	Thomas Race
340	Tenter Close	Charles Alderson	Thomas Race
310	Marle Close	Charles Alderson	Thomas Race

Stenkrith Mill, based on a nineteenth drawing by Thomas Fawcett. At this stage probably modified to a corn mill from an earlier fulling mill.

Drawing by Jane Tilley.

Up river at Stenkrith Bridge (south side) on the B6259 where the bridge has been constructed to enable the river Eden to flow into rock fissures which by-pass the main waterfall and flow separately into Stenkrith Park.

Close-up of Stenkrith Bridge (south side).

The hydro-electric station on the north side of Stenkrith Bridge built circa 1902/3 and now demolished.
A note in the Yorkshire Evening Post of April 23rd 1902 stated: The Kirkby Stephen Parish Council
have entered a strong protest against the erection by the North-Eastern Railway Company of an electric
generating station by the side of the River Eden at Stenkrith close to the picturesque falls and scenery known as
Coopkarnal. One councillor observed that it would be a grievous hardship if visitors who had long frequented
the spot were to go and find it turned into a mill. There was already one mill in Stenkrith, understood to be
turned by the devil, and the second one, now in course of construction was in close alliance.

In Stenkrith Park traces remain of a banked mill race that probably powered the mill .

By way of an end note to this chapter the presence of the massive engineering project which culminated in the Stainmore railway will be mentioned. The line passed above Stenkrith Park on the south bank of the river Eden, The road bridge itself was redesigned to accommodate the railway across the river. Kirkby Stephen acted as the operating centre for the western section of the Stainmore line and as a junction for lines to Tebay and Penrith. It had an engine shed for a dozen locomotives. Heavy trains over Stainmore summit needed "banking" with a second locomotive assisting from the rear. There were various attempts to create a cross-Pennine rail link which began early in the nineteenth century. One diffi culty was landowners such as the Duke of Cleveland who refused permission to cross his land east of Barnard Castle in 1839. A scheme in the 1840's fi nally received approval but was abandoned in spite of permission from the Duke who had extracted a high price for the land designated for the route. One diffi culty for a cross- Pennine project had been to fi nd a reason to link early rail development on the eastern seaboard of northern England with the west coast in view of the barren land of the Pennines. This was achieved once there was a connection established between the South Durham coalfi eld and the rich iron-ore mines around Barrow-in-Furness. It created a durable link for the massive iron and steel industries of these two areas. Coal and coke passed to the west and haematite ore travelling in the opposite direction was used to upgrade low quality Cleveland iron ores. The South Durham & Lancashire Union Railway (SDLUR) scheme was passed in 1857 for the construction of a 44 mile line. It opened in 1861 and ran from Co Durham over Stainmore to Kirkby Stephen and continued to join the west coast line at Tebay. The line became part of the Stockton & Darlington Railway which was taken over by the North Eastern Railway in 1863. Sixty years later the NER was amalgamated into the London & North Eastern Railway (LNER). Whilst the original catalyst for the line was freight it soon carried passengers. The Eden Valley Railway opened as a branch line in 1862 to connect Kirkby Stephen with Penrith and Appleby. The project was famous for its viaducts built in stone and iron; Belah, Merrygill, Mousegill, Podgill and Smardale. The Belah viaduct was an outstanding engineering achievement crossing the deep gill of the river Belah; 1000 feet long and 200 feet above the valley. Designed by Thomas Bouch the bridge structure was pre- fabricated iron with stone piers at either side of the valley. Unfortunately its lightweight construction placed limits on locomotive size on the steep gradients of this heavily used line. The Kirkby Stephen to Tebay line closed to passengers in 1952 but remained open for freight. The last of the Barrow works reliant on Durham coke closed in 1961 and in 1962 the line closed to all traffic.

Chapter Six: References

The Transactions of the Cumberland & Westmorland Antiquarian & Archaeological Society Series One, Two & Three have been abbreviated to CW1, 2 or 3

1.   From Daniel Defoe, *A tour through the whole island of Great Britain* (London, 1724 - 7), Letter 8 Part 4. Quoted in Marie Hartley & Joan Ingilby, *The old hand-knitters of the Dales* (Clapham, 1988), p.25 where the authors go on to state that there is no reason to suppose that the beginnings of the stocking trade arose in Westmorland given the ubiquity of this trade across many parts of England.

2.   Christopher Hill, *Economic problems of the church.* (Oxford, 1956) The author notes that there is no general agreement about the social effects of the *plunder of the church* or that it went mainly to the gentry. The greatest beneficiary may have been the lay landowning class or at least its bankrupt section. But Hill notes that after Henry VIII the process of spoliation continued under succeeding monarchs and lay the foundations for a fascination with wealth creation which spread slowly down the social hierarchy.

3.   C.M.L. Bouch & G. P. Jones, *The Lake Counties 1500 - 1830. A social & economic history* (Manchester, 1961), chapter 4.

4.   J.D. Marshall, 'Agrarian wealth and social structure in pre-industrial Cumbria', *Economic History Review*, 33/4, 503 - 521.

5.   C.E. Searle, 'Cumbria's parliamentary enclosure movement: A comparative case study of rural quiescence', *CW2*, 1995, 247 - 269.

6.   J.V. Beckett, 'Absentee landownership in the later seventeenth and early eighteenth centuries. The case of Cumbria', *Northern History*, 1983, 87 - 107.

7.   M.E. Shepherd, *Across the oceans: Emigration from Cumberland and Westmorland before 1914*, (Carlisle, 2011) p. 170.

8.   Quoted in E.J.T. Collins (ed.), *The agrarian history of England and Wales vol. 7, 1850-1914 Part 1,* p.402.

9.   Marshall, 'Agrarian wealth..' op. cit. p. 514.

10. Loraine Ashcroft, *Vital Statistics: The Westmorland 'Census' of 1787.* (Curwen Archive Trust, 1992).

11. Lesley O'Connell Edwards, 'Working hand knitters in England from the sixteenth to the nineteenth centuries', *Textile History*, 41 (1), May 2010, p. 75.

12. Robert Southey, 'A true story of the terrible knitters e'Dent...' *The Doctor*, Volume 7, Chapter XXIV. (1834). The story is referred to in Adam Sedgwick, *A memorial by the trustees of Cowgill Chapel* (Cambridge, 1868) and reprinted by Hollett and Boulton, (Sedbergh and Dent, 1984).

13.   Joan Thirsk, *Economic policy and projects: The development of a consumer society in early modern England.* (Oxford, 1978), p. 5.

14.   ibid. p. 45.

15.   Marie Hartley and Joan Ingilby, *The Old Hand-Knitters of the Dales.* (Clapham, 1951).

16.   Lesley O'Connell Edwards, 'Working Hand Knitters in England from the Sixteenth to the Nineteenth Centuries', *Textile History*, 41 (1), p.71.

17.   ibid. p.73.

18.   Quoted in Marshall, 'Agrarian wealth..' p.514. Cumbria Archive Centre, Carlisle under the name Richard Dickson of Nateby: PROB/1678/AINVX17.

In relation to stocking knitting Gowling also mentions Vincent Powson of Nateby who died in 1670 whose most valuable assets were stockings, *wool and yarn valued at 12s*. Later noting that Powson had debts from seven men to whom he may have supplied knitting yarn. See Margaret Gowling, *Kirkby Stephen in 1605: A Westmorland village in the seventeenth century.* (Kirkby Stephen, 2000), p. 29.

19.   G.L. Gomme (ed.), *The Gentleman's Magazine Library: being a classified collection of the chief contents from 1731 to 1868.* (London, 1901). p. 154.

20.   Hartley and Ingilby, op. cit., facing page 68.

21.   Arthur Young, *A six months tour through the north of England.* Volume 3, letter XVII. (London, 1770).

22.   Rev. W. Nicholls, *The history and traditions of Mallerstang Forest and Pendragon Castle.* (Manchester, 1883), p. 99 - 100.

23.   T. S. Willan, *An eighteenth-century shopkeeper: Abraham Dent of Kirkby Stephen.* (Manchester, 1970). T. S. Willan (1910 - 1994) became Professor of Economic History at The University of Manchester.

24.   ibid. p. 61.

25.   ibid. p. 60.

26.   G. Elliott, 'The decline of the woollen trade in Cumberland, Westmorland and Northumberland in the late sixteenth century'. *CW2*, lxi (1961), p. 112 - 119.

27.   ibid. p. 119.

28.   Willan, op cit, p. 70.

29.   ibid. p. 66.

30.   ibid. p. 72. The majority of Dent's stockings were sold to two army contractors in London apparently *undyed*.

31. ibid. p. 60. The reference is to Sir Daniel Fleming in 1671: and the market in this Towne (of Kirkby Stephen) *is much improved by the trade of stockings, lately taken up and made in this Towne and parts adjacent.*

32. ibid. p. 61 for Barnett and p. 67 for Fawcett.

33. ibid. p.61.

34. John F. Curwen, *The later records relating to North Westmorland or the Barony of Appleby.* (Kendal, 1932), p. 7.

35. ibid. p. 133.

36. Anne M. A. Anderson and Alec Swailes, *Kirkby Stephen* (Kirkby Stephen, 1985), p. 47.

37. M. Davies-Shiel, 'The Kirkby Stephen and Hartley watermills' in *May Walk 1981: Hartley Area* a pamphlet published by the Cumberland and Westmorland Antiquarian and Archaeological Society, p. 1 - 2.

38. There is a useful discussion of the Faraday background in James F. Riley, *The hammer and the anvil: A background to Michael Faraday* (Clapham, 1954) chapters 4 and 5. This book also lists some useful source material from local newspapers at this time including articles by Kirkby Stephen teacher and historian, F. W. Parrott: 'Famous scientist's links with Westmorland' in *Cumberland and Westmorland Herald*, February 24th, 1951. March 3rd, 1951 and March 10th, 1951. Other articles 'The Faradays' in *Penrith* Observer, January 23rd, 1951 and February 13th, 1951.

39. Will of Richard Faraday, wool spinner of Kirkby Stephen. Cumbria Archive Centre, Carlisle. 1816/W565.

40. *The Faraday Geneaology published on the occasion of the Death of Michael Faraday* by J. E. Faraday is held by The Royal Institution. Reference: RI MS F/10).

41. Cumbria Archive Centre, Kendal. Appleby Sessions Roll. WQ/SR/613/17.

42. The efforts to introduce manufacturing into the town did not go unnoticed. The Kendal Mercury reported in a 'Guide to Kirkby Stephen and its environs' on January 20th 1849 that in the early nineteenth century "the building called the factory, was erected by Messrs Greaves and Co. for a cotton mill, and after the same was put in operation a large number of the boys and girls of the town were employed therein, and money as a natural consequence, was more freely circulated. Coeval with the factory was Aselbie's celebrated academy, but both these establishments ultimately went down, and Kirkby ever since has been left to its usual resources." Another cotton mill had been erected at Yosgill, Brough and on May 11th 1894 The Manchester Weekly Times commented: "Manchester people have a peculiar interest in Brough owing to the fact that about a century ago an attempt was made to establish the cotton spinning industry there. A local magnate built a mill,

and it was not his fault that Manchester, and not Brough, became cottonopolis." *Parkinson's guide and history of Kirkby Stephen and district* (Kirkby Stephen, c.1920) mentions that "At the beginning of the 19th century this building was erected (East Ward Union Institution) as a cotton mill by Messrs. Graves, Lane and Co. who became bankrupts about the year 1810."

43. *Kirkby Stephen & Appleby Monthly Messenger*, July 1891.

44. Cumbria Archive Centre, Kendal. Kirkby Stephen Tithe Map. WDRC/8/169.

45. "The first person who settled in this town (of Kirkby Stephen) who, in my opinion, was legitimately entitled to be denominated a manufacturer, was a person named Titley - a manufacturer of coarse wool hats." *Kendal Mercury*, January 20th 1849. According to this article this was about the same time as the establishment of the cotton factory - see note 42.

46. It may be of interest to note that one of Strutt's sixth generation descendants, John Herbert Strutt (1935 - 2010), came to purchase the 600-acre Hartley Fold estate just outside Kirkby Stephen town in the 1960's.

47. R. S. Fitton & A. P. Wadsworth, *The Strutts and the Arkwrights 1758 - 1830. A study of the early factory system.* (Manchester, 1958), p. 60.

48. *Extracts from the Court Roll of the Manor of Kirkby Stephen of admissions to certain premises now the Factory, 1747 - 1809.* Cumbria Archive Centre, Kendal. WC/C/OL743.

49. It would seem that this lack of evidence is not unusual judging by the comment made about Richard Arkwright: *We know much less of Arkwright than we do of Strutt; he remains one of the biographical enigmas of the eighteenth century. The authenticated facts about his life before his rise to fame are meagre; even his family could not recover many.* Fitton & Wadsworth, op cit, p. 60.

50. A useful and thorough online history of Peter Degraves' life including the dubious circumstances of his emigration to Australia is: Gregory Jefferys, 'Hugh Macintosh & Peter Degraves: The story of an officer and a gentleman'. *eprints.utas.edu.au/11730/1/jefferys.pdf.*

51. The personal estate and effects of John Dand sold as a result of his bankruptcy in 1809 involving the bargain sale of goods and chattels at The Manufactory and Stenkrith Mill. Cumbria Archive Centre, Kendal. WC/C/OL743/1. John Dand had purchased The Manufactory from George Dickenson in 1807 and the building was subsequently sold to Richard Binks in 1810. Binks leased the building to The Visitor & Guardians of the Poor of Kirkby Stephen in 1818.

52. An important article describing this medieval cloth industry including the process of fulling is E. M. Carus-Wilson, 'An industrial revolution of the thirteenth century'. *Economic History Review*, XI, 1941, pp 39 - 60.

53. 'Ancient Corn Mills: North Westmorland's Silent Mill Wheels' from *The Herald*, 31.10.1942 provides a useful survey by local author J. Walker Nicholson. It is interesting to note the comment for the mill at 'Kirkby Stephen, Nateby and Wharton' as follows: *It stood at Stenkrith, the site being covered by the present railway embankment. There has also been a woollen mill on the opposite side of the Eden, and the adjoining field is still called Tenter Hill. Later oatmeal was made at this mill which was dismantled soon after 1860.*

Chapter 7

Thomas Fawcett's Sketchbook

The title page of the sketchbook

Introduction to the sketchbook of Thomas Fawcett

Some of the drawings of the town of Kirkby Stephen contained in Thomas Fawcett's (1812 - 1891) sketchbook appear in the pages that follow. Indeed, one of the drawings of Market Street identifies the house he was born in - next door to the Black Bull Inn. There is an important predecessor in the publication history of the Fawcett drawings because many appeared in the book *Kirkby Stephen* by Anne M.A. Anderson and Alec Swailes in 1985. This remarkable volume also contained valuable historical notes about Kirkby Stephen district and an important set of drawings by Anne Anderson of the town at the time the book was published.

Thomas Fawcett's mother died when he was about ten years old. He was first employed in training horses 'for the race' and at the age of thirteen his father apprenticed him to learn to plaster and paint. In 1833 he went to Liverpool to learn stained glass work and returned to Kirkby Stephen in 1834. It has been suggested that in his early years Thomas lead a reckless life but following his return to Kirkby Stephen he married*, started in business for himself and joined the Wesleyan Society (Methodists). The sketchbook was created in later life but it would seem that some drawings were created earlier and from the perspective of his memory of the town as a young boy in 1817. Many of the sketchbook drawings are so dated but were actually created later. This helps to account for the variety of datings that appear in the drawings. It is apparent that there were other drawings too. One is *The Stocking Market* which is included in Chapter Six and a drawing of Stenkrith Mill for which there is a modern illustration here based on a crude photograph of the original. The current whereabouts of the original is unknown. Perhaps there are other drawings yet to be discovered. Thomas Fawcett mapped the town buildings very accurately probably using the large scale Ordnance Survey sheets that began to appear in 1860's. His original map of the town in the sketchbook is not included here but each property was numbered and from this Fawcett identified each property by number and by occupant. The sketchbook drawings are accompanied by poems - a popular pastime of that period. There were other poets in the town (Poet Close and Joe Steel for example) and they probably stimulated each other with their verses.

Thomas Fawcett was born in an age of a rapidly expanding road network and a number of drawings include a stagecoach. In later life he must have been aware of the frenetic development of the railways because two major networks were to dominate the town from the 1860's. We do not know his response to the railway revolution but perhaps his use of memory to create scenes of the town from his boyhood suggest an attachment to a slower, pastoral way of life.

The Fawcett Sketchbook is now with Cumbria Archive Service, Kendal. Ref: WDX 1137/1

*A handwritten note in the Fawcett papers possibly written by a grandson states that Thomas met his future wife (Esther Bailiff of Crosby Garrett) at a corn mill on the river Belah when he was seventeen and she two years his junior. These papers (headed 'Old Water Mills): Cumbria Archive Centre, Kendal: WDX 1137/2.

William Coats' house on what is now North Road called Sparrow Hall. On this site there is now a walled garden next to the garage. The drawing is accompanied by a poem and the first verse reads:

This old thatched cot that used to stand
In bygone days upon some land
Was called the Sparrow Hall
Those birds did build their nests in thatch
Were numerous when the young they hatched
And hence their brood forestall

Between the Parish Church and Low Mill is an area variously called The Green, North Road or Union Square. The original houses are set back with gardens down to the river and there has since been infill with newer properties. Probably by at least the eighteenth century it became an area used by craftsmen and also became the site of the Union Cotton Mill. In the early nineteenth century the drawing depicts the stocks which occupied the middle of The Green. The drawing also refers to this area as Tinkler Hill.

This fine drawing of bull baiting on Market Square illustrates how little has changed since in respect of architecture. The Old Brewery (now a newsagents) operated as Braithwaite's in the nineteenth century printing the Kirkby Stephen Monthly Messenger and now has an additional storey. The Cloisters were built on the instructions of John Waller Esq. in 1810. The shop to the left is shown with a first storey spinning gallery.

The east side of upper Market Street from Little Wiend to the narrow entrance to Royal Arcade shows the great changes that occurred later in the nineteenth century. The properties on the left became substantial town houses (now with shops to the ground floor). Number 7 is drawn as 'Bainbridge's New Inn' which has altered the least.

Continuing the line of buildings on upper Market Street from what is now HSBC bank. These buildings were again replaced with fine town houses in the nineteenth century.

The west side of upper Market Street or Fletcher Hill. The house on the left (33) is noted as Sally Birkbeck's house whilst 34 and 35 were probably replaced by the Methodist Chapel (then a Youth Hostel) and Fletcher House. The property on the right (36) stands at the entrance to Croft Street. The poem attached to the drawing is worth noting because of its reference to knitted stockings (overleaf).

Nanny Coats & Paupers Bell

Old Nanny Coats who lived in town,
A person known quite well;
She used to wear a linsay gown
And rung the paupers bell.

This burly woman as appears,
By homely fare was fed,
Part living got when old in years,
By tolling bell for't dead.

But knitting there was in demand,
For stockings that were sold;
And all of them were knitt by hand,
By men and women old.

Their scanty pittance thus was got,
For winter nights so long,
Some times a cup of tea from't pot,
And often not so strong.

Then tea was tea, in former days,
'Twas seven shillings a pound;
Folks had to scheme in many ways,
It made them look a round.

Yet after all 'twas no disgrace,
For Coats to ring the bell,
Its only few in't present race,
Could do the job as well.

On the west side of Market Street there is a long run of recognisable properties which cover the following pages (39 to 50) and beyond. Thomas Fawcett identifies the house where he was born next door to the Black Bull Inn. Attached to the drawing is the poem 'Old Coaching Days' included overleaf.

Old Coaching Days

What changes there have taken place,
In the last sixty years;
In olden times with coaches race,
But all these disappear.

When we were lads there stood behind,
The guard with long tin horn;
Whose thrilling blast did us remind,
How passengers were borne.

Through fertile dales and wild Stainmore
The merry groups did go;
In Eymouths coach with horses four,
Through sunshine and through snow.

And many a queer tale was told,
While sitting side by side;
With passengers both young and old,
Who on the coach did ride.

Such scenes as these have pass'd away,
And many more beside,
Old Billy Warbreck's had his day,
And Thomas Heavyside.

These gallant men drove four in hand,
Through Kirkby Stephen town;
From Spittlehead through Westmorland
Earn'd many a half crown.

The sequence of numbers here is incorrect but W. Dickinson's house is followed by the Crown Inn (41) and at 42 the Red Lion (modern day antique shop).

The perambulation down Market Street continues and the Red Lion is again represented followed by Croft House.

Continuing north down Market Street facing the Square the outline of buildings is again little changed.

On Market Street, The Shambles is the middle property (52).

Upper Market Street and Mr Powley's (now a three storey Kings Arms Hotel).

The next building on from Mr Powley's was replaced with what finally became a bank.

Townhead House on High Street.

Group of thatch't houses on Primrose Hill.

Blacklins Old Corn and Saw Mill on Riverside.

A view of Sower Pow - an area round the old Post Office - looking towards Market Street. It is clearly an area used by craftsmen - a brewery, malthouse, tanyard and stabling are all included in Fawcett's description.

Chapter 8

Upper Eden Upland: Introduction

Abandoned stone trough at High Brae, Mallerstang Edge

This introduction provides a brief description of the geology and topography of an upland landscape. The chapters that follow continue with a more detailed topography and an outline of the small scale mineral extraction and quarrying that occurred in the area.

It has been suggested in the main introduction that the upper Eden valley retains a distinct historical identity. The whole area forms a broad horseshoe of upland mostly of unenclosed common, rising on either side of the valley from Eden's source at the southern end of Mallerstang. Here it also coincides with the southern boundary of Cumbria and the northern edge of the Yorkshire Dales National Park. This upland is the geographical boundary of the Eden watershed but some exceptions have been made to include some outlying ground beyond it which can be said to form part of a larger cultural unit. A case in point is the exposed limestone of The Clouds and forming part of Ravenstonedale Common. This is a remarkable area on the lower western slopes of Wild Boar Fell where the coalescence of culture and nature is most striking. A combination of enclosed and unenclosed grazing alongside spectacular limestone outcropping. The Clouds has been extensively worked for lead and the scars formed by this extraction have been re-absorbed into the landscape. The inclusion of this area is given additional coherence by the shared religious and political history of the parishes of Grisedale, Mallerstang and Ravenstonedale.

With regard to topography the points of maximum height - moving clockwise - are; Nine Standards Rigg (662m) on Hartley Fell, High Seat (709m) and Hugh Seat (689m) on Mallerstang Edge and, after crossing the watershed at Aisgill, Swarth Fell (681m), Wild Boar Fell (708m), Little Fell (559m) and Clouds (468m). In terms of a broader topography it is a commonplace to note that the high tops under consideration here border a vast area of wild and open country - great tracts of wilderness which extend particularly north and east across the Pennines and Cross Fell into County Durham, Teesdale and the Yorkshire Dales. The area contains the source of four major rivers; Lune, Eden, Swale and Ure. Indeed there is a continuous valley formed by Eden and Ure which was remarked on by early geologists such that the Pennine range could be traversed in this one narrow valley from east to west coast, from Humber to Solway. Both rivers rise from head waters on the eastern flank of the valley at the southern end of Mallerstang.

There is evidence of mining activity, particularly for coal and lead, in most parts of this carboniferous upland. Greater detail about the location of some of the most significant sites is provided in each chapter but some more general comments about mineral extraction and geology will be made here. The geology of the area is complex and, to oversimplify, consists of high fell tops capped mostly by millstone grit overlaying limestones and shales. From within the limestone series lead has been sought across a huge area described by geologists as the Northern Pennine Orefield which extends from Hadrian's Wall in the north to the Craven upland around Settle in Yorkshire. A variety of minerals have been extracted including silver, copper, lead, tin and also coal. In Eden pockets of mineralisation are evident from faulting that occurs south of Stainmore which can be traced from Augill near Brough (where lead was smelted) to Longrigg and Hartley Birkett (where the limestone series is particularly complex and faulted), Ladthwaite, Dalefoot and Great Bell in Mallerstang, Fothergill Sike (close to the Settle - Carlisle rail tunnel at Birkett) and Clouds in Ravenstonedale. Limestones also crop out

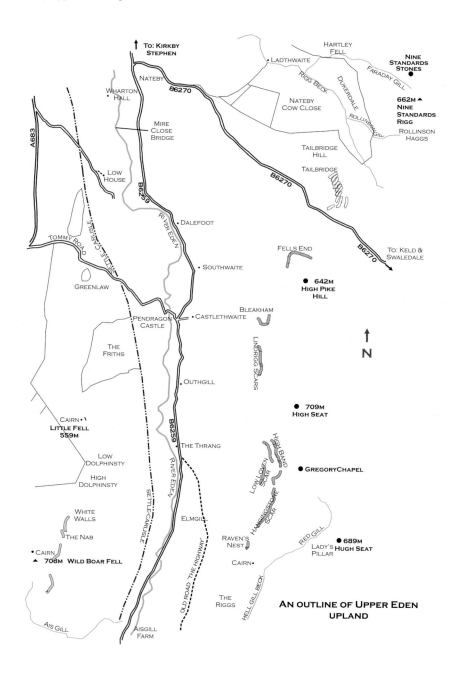

An outline of Upper Eden upland

along the flanks of the upland valley of Dukerdale and in all these places there are traces of (principally) lead mining activity.

However, lead mining was never of major importance in upper Eden in spite of the rash of workings across the area. The yield from deposits was always small in comparison with higher production areas at Alston, Swaledale, Grassington and, in the Eden valley itself, at Dufton and Hilton on the Pennine edge east of Appleby. Men were attracted into the Pennine orefield from late medieval times with prospects of work either as individuals or in small partnerships. They worked in remote places where smelt mills developed - such as those at Augill, Hartley Birkett and at Aisgill in Mallerstang. Landowners were instrumental in extracting value from their land both above and below ground and this process gained momentum in the seventeenth and eighteenth centuries as the Industrial Revolution gathered pace and demand for raw materials accelerated. By the 1840's the UK was the world's largest producer of lead and it was from this time that a new 'economic geology' was used in mapping the orefields and which resulted in a string of Geological Surveys beginning in the 1870's. In 1891 a memoir *The Geology of the Country around Mallerstang* was published. The lead industry suffered from the later 1870's when imported lead with a higher silver content replaced local ores. The London Lead Company operated mines at Alston and Nenthead and mines in Westmorland and Teesdale. The company closed in 1905 although local mining did continue. Greenside lead mine at the head of Ullswater survived until the middle of the twentieth century.

With regard to coal it would seem that although the Romans worked both coal and lead there was a long gap until about the thirteenth century before coal started to be used again for heating in monasteries and castles. The usual fuel had been wood which was also used for charcoal in lead smelting at least until supply began to dwindle. There were more significant reserves of coal on Stainmore compared to Mallerstang and by the early nineteenth century some farmers had a second occupation in coal mining and more became fully employed. By the middle of the century it is estimated that one third of the male working population in Stainmore were miners. Coal mining was affected by the railway and Durham coal and by 1891 most extraction in Eden had been lost. At the same time coal had been sought for lime burning because of the proximity of both limestone and coal. The end product was used in mortar and as fertiliser in agriculture.

Although difficult to quantify exactly it has been estimated that there are over one million acres of common land in Britain. Today, over 25% of the land area of the old county of Westmorland, including much of the southern portion of the Eden valley, remains as unenclosed common. In general terms the upland landscape of upper Eden provides, as a result of its higher elevation, a feeling of spaciousness which is probably enhanced by the absence of enclosure. In earlier times this ground had been manorial waste and remained relatively undisturbed even during periods of rapid change - for example during the parliamentary enclosure movement in the eighteenth and nineteenth centuries. (The landscape was, of course, partially disturbed by the industrial revolution because of mining and quarrying activity. However, much of this small scale activity is poorly documented and surface features can be hard to date accurately). In the case of upper Eden much of the enclosure that did occur was in fact done piecemeal in an earlier period between 1550 - 1750 and by private agreement. In Mallerstang many of the field enclosures in the valley bottom are probably of earlier date. These earlier field patterns tended to be small and irregular compared to the large, rectangular fields created under act of Parliament.

Otherwise only a very small portion of upland was enclosed in upper Eden south or east of Kirkby Stephen during the period of parliamentary enclosure in the period 1770 - 1890. The exception was the enclosure on the western flank of Little Fell on Kirkby Stephen Common which was only finally created in the mid-nineteenth century following a boundary dispute. *The Friths*, an enclosure north of Little Fell is identified as a much earlier medieval cattle enclosure or *vaccary* attached to Pendragon Castle. In the wider area there was considerable parliamentary enclosure of upland waste in part associated with competition between two major landowners; the earls of Lonsdale (Lowther) and Thanet (formerly the Clifford family, earls of Cumberland). In the late eighteenth century both families were developing their estates. The reason why this rivalry did not extend to upper Eden might lie in the poor quality of the land and the cost of enclosure. Another feature which has been regarded as a restriction on the gentry during the age of agricultural improvement was the system of land tenure known as customary tenant right which gave rights of inheritance over property. It was originally linked to a form of military obligation imposed on tenants to give service on the Anglo-Scottish border. These conditions evolved to give greater security to tenants. During the changes of the sixteenth century tenants held on to these privileges and resisted landowner attempts to force them to accept leases on their property. The result was to prevent manorial lords controlling tenanted land because they could not purchase it. Tenants were able to exercise rights over the process of enclosure and they could also initiate enclosure if it was in their interest to do so. One case of opposition to enclosure occurred in 1767 when Ravenstonedale tenants opposed the lord of the manor (Sir James Lowther) in his attempt to enclose the common. However, in general terms manorial wastes provided the basis for a relationship between landowner and commoner which formed a community of interest and use. The landowner owned the soil and minerals but his share of other products; pasture for grazing, peat, wood and stone was shared with others living in the community. Often the extent of these rights depended, for example in the case of a tenant, on the amount of land they occupied. In fact these rights and the exercise of manorial customs was closely controlled and administered by manor courts under the jurisdiction of landowners. Nor did the commons originally provide for a right of access to the public - a development that was to come much later and only once the system of manorial courts had broken down and public interest began to be recognised. In the latter part of the nineteenth century the enclosure movement had created concern about how little land had been set aside for recreation. It has been said that the appreciation of the upland wastes as a natural landscape suitable for recreation coincided with the development of a more intensive agriculture which depended on enclosure. What remains of the old manorial upland waste has been described by Oliver Rackham in *The History of the Countryside* as ancient countryside used for rough grazing in strong contrast to the modern planned countryside of enclosed farmland in the valleys.

Chapter 9

Upper Eden Upland: Hartley Fell & Nine Standards

Hartley Birkett on Hartley Fell:
The hill has been heavily exploited for lead.

Edward II granted Hartley Castle to Sir Andrew de Harcla in about 1315 and it continued to be subject to frequent destruction by Scots raiding parties. Possession passed to Ralph Nevil (or Ranulph dc Nevill) of Raby who sold it to Sir Thomas de Musgrave. Musgrave built a stone tower in 1353. Later Musgraves were to enlarge the fortress into a mansion.

However, the Musgrave family chose to relocate to Edenhall and deserted Hartley Castle leaving it to fall into ruin and to be demolished by Sir Christopher Musgrave who died in 1735. The drawing by Samuel and Nathaniel Buck is dated 1739. The site is now a private house.

This chapter focuses on Hartley Birkett, Hartley Fell, Nine Standards and Tailbridge. In general terms the area consists of unenclosed moorland with gently rising ground to the east which features exposed limestone on the lower slopes culminating in a series of gritstone outcrops as the watershed is approached. It is wild and open country given additional emphasis by its continuation beyond the watershed into the adjoining areas of Durham, Teesdale and North Yorkshire. In brief the notable landscape features are an exposed ridge of limestone at Longrigg

Enlarged view of the lower right section of the Hartley Castle engraving. The detail consists of an elevated view from the castle down to the river Eden and Kirkby Stephen's parish church. Whether the bridge was drawn from memory is not clear but if it was intended to be Frank's Bridge then it is evident that it is misrepresented because the river bends sharply to the right at this point which is not depicted in the drawing. In reality the bridge is also located much closer to the town.

and Little Longrigg which lie adjacent to the great dome of limestone at Hartley Birkett. This is the location for extensive lead mining in the past and can be described, quite accurately, as a post-industrial landscape. On the watershed are the enigmatic *Nine Standards* and to the south the attractive and isolated upland valley of Dukerdale. To the south again, adjoining the B6270 to Swaledale, is Tailbridge which is a vast expanse of limestone with its surface exposed as pavement on its eastern flank. There is a summit cairn to the west on Tailbridge Hill.

As mentioned there is extensive evidence of lead mining in the vicinity of Hartley Birkett and also trials for copper. Coal was sought on the flanks of Hartley Fell amongst the gritstone levels of Greyrigg and Greenside. There has also been quarrying. Primitive shelters and sheepfolds dot these outcrops, past refuges for both man and livestock.

The Hartley Birkett veins and lead workings are located at an outcropping of limestone east of the fell road that climbs south-east from Hartley village. The hill of Hartley Birkett consists of a massive layer of faulted limestone and has the appearance of comprehensive exploitation. There was a smelt mill at the northern end of the hill although only traces of the buildings now remain. The Hartley Birkett mine operated in a relatively small way working mainly low grade ore probably in the period 1717 - 1881 although records indicate mining activity at *Harcla* as early as the fourteenth century. To the east of Hartley Birkett there are visible traces

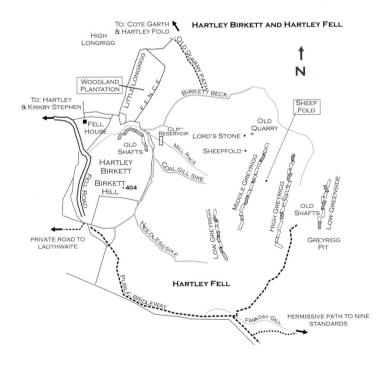

of the mill race described on the first edition 6 inch Ordnance Survey map (1862). The race was sourced from Coalgill Sike below Greyrigg which in turn fed mill dams at a lower level. One dam, although overgrown, is still in place. A substantial section of the centre portion of Hartley Birkett has been hushed and excavated. There are the remains of numerous shafts on the hill, dressing floors, hushes and a reservoir. The mineral rights were held by the Musgrave estate who originally resided at Hartley Castle until 1697 when they relocated to Edenhall. The Musgraves demolished the castle and the stone reused to build the farm which now occupies the site. There are some records of contracts created in the 1750's which extended leases and agreed the location of new shafts to be worked. Agreements specified the price of ore and provided for its washing at Birkett. This was an active period for mining and for landowners to take full advantage of their mineral rights. In 1746 - 7 one John Birkbeck and others of Hartley were accused of polluting the streams of Hartley Town beck by hushing for lead ore. In 1755 John Langstaff was fined one shilling for the same offence. In the period 1758 - 61 lead from Birkett had duty paid by a Thomas Parke & Co.. It has been noted in an earlier chapter that documentary evidence for many of these small scale enterprises is hard to find. T.S. Willan in *An Eighteenth Century Shopkeeper: Abraham Dent of Kirkby Stephen* commented how difficult it was to trace the industrial occupations of townspeople but notes one record of a David Harker of Hartley, a boy of thirteen, killed by falling down a shaft at a lead mine on Hartley Fell in 1772. Willan also notes that whilst there are some records of miners residing in Kirkby Stephen in this period mining was never regarded as an important activity. Some documents are retained in the Musgrave archives in Carlisle and Kendal. In the second half of the nineteenth century the Pease family of Darlington seem to have taken an interest in mining in the area. Mineral statistics, published in 1983, for the period 1845 - 1913 indicated that the Henry Pease company controlled the mine from 1870 - 1881 producing both lead and silver in modest quantities under the management of John Cain. Henry Pease was a Quaker group with a strong interest in railways in the north-east. They had pioneered the Stockton & Darlington railway and later constructed the Stainmore line. They also had interests in mining - the Stainmore traffic was designed originally to carry haematite iron ore from Furness to Teeside - with coke and coal moving in the opposite direction to feed iron works at Barrow. The Hartley Birkett vein extended south towards Ladthwaite and was also worked. Just north of Hartley Birkett both lead and copper were mined on what is now fellside pasture below the limestone scars of Little Longrigg and High Longrigg. Iron ore was also extracted here during the 1880's in significant quantities.

Hartley Birkett from the first edition six inch to one mile Ordnance Survey sheet XXIII East Ward, 1862. (Not to scale). Cumbria Archive Centre, Kendal.

Lord's Stone - a large boulder on the gritstone outcrops of Greyrigg just south of Birkett Beck and adjacent to stone quarries. Both natural markings and with carved names, initials and dates. Also identified as a boundary stone between the parishes of Winton and Hartley. The earliest mark is said to be ST1730 referring to the landowner Sackville Tufton.

Coal was also sought in various locations in this area evident from the early large scale Ordnance Survey mapping but also attested by the naming of streams such as Coalgill Sike which drains west to Hartley Birkett. There are old coal pits east of High Greyrigg and, south of Nine Standards, the remains of Rollinson Colliery which began to be worked in the eighteenth century. Some colliery accounts from the Musgrave archive in Carlisle dated 1729 - 1732 would be consistent with operation at a time when it was difficult to bring fuel into the area. The few bridleways marked on modern maps confirm the routes taken by quarrymen and colliers working these higher fells.

The Nine Standards on Hartley Fell. These enigmatic pillar cairns continue to challenge us about their origin and purpose. Not located at the highest point on the ridge (where there is a trig point) they are nevertheless visible from miles around. Some of the cairns were rebuilt . 2006.

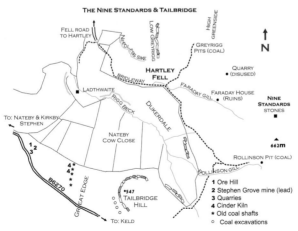

The key (above right) indicates the mine & quarry sites shown on the First Edition six inch to one mile Ordnance Survey sheet 1862. Further coal shafts spill over the B6270 in the vicinity of Great Edge

Before moving on to the Nine Standards brief mention will be made of the topographical references in this area which use the name *Faraday*. The subject of Michael Faraday known as 'the father of electricity' and the context of his humble family origins in Yorkshire and Westmorland has been dealt with in Chapter 6. Here it is only necessary to mention Faraday Gill which is a narrow beck running west across Hartley Fell from the Nine Standards. Wainwright's Coast to Coast route passes on its southern bank and it also passes what is now a pile of stones identified on the first edition six inch Ordnance Survey sheet (1862) as Faraday House, but even then was described as a ruin. There is a speculation that these landmarks are named after the Richard Faraday who became a prosperous man of business in Kirkby Stephen with interests in slate as well as textiles. Richard was Michael's uncle whereas Michael's father (James) moved on from Kirkby Stephen to settle in London where Michael Faraday was born. There is also a disused quarry some few hundred metres north which has also been suggested to have Faraday connections by Dr Bence Jones an early Faraday biographer. These suppositions were also mentioned by the local historian F W Parrott who wrote a series of newspaper articles in the early 1950's about the Faraday connection with the Sandemanian religious sect.

The history of the Nine Standards - a series of dry-stone pillar cairns which became Grade II Listed in 1984 - is both interesting and enigmatic. An archaeological survey was published in 2005 and they have since been re-built. The Standards are a local monument and are visible for miles around. Their role has been variously described as boundary marker between the old county of Westmorland and Yorkshire, to fool marauding Scots or as a shepherd's meeting place. Many of the claimed sources documenting their origin have proved difficult to confirm. The cairns did eventually come to mark the boundary between the parishes of Winton and Hartley although it appears this was a matter of convenience rather than design. It has also been suggested that their construction had something to do with the Musgrave family who were the principal landowners up to at least 1937. On balance it would seem that the Nine Standards do have a history stretching into antiquity but most probably underwent modification. With regard to territorial boundaries it is clear that there was an element of fluidity in these remote areas as early mappings indicate. Hodgson's Map of Westmorland (1829) defines some of this no- man's land particularly on Tailbridge and Mallerstang as *disputed ground*. The watershed of this area would have been an interface between three rival estates all of which would have had a strong interest in asserting their claims to mineral rights. In addition there were disputes over sheep grazing particularly when the enclosure movement gathered pace and from the eighteenth century there was intense rivalry about territory. Perambulations over disputed ground were not uncommon and were conducted to provide confirmation of parish boundaries particularly where a watershed was indistinct. Later in the nineteenth century these were often advertised in the local press.

There were searches for lead at Dukerdale on the high west-facing fells and also below Coldbergh Scar at Dukerdale Head but they do not seem to have amounted to much. Tailbridge, on lower ground, is an attractive area with some limestone pavement and is also the crossing point of the B6270 between Kirkby Stephen and Swaledale. It is here that there was meeting ground for the three major estates in this portion of Westmorland.

The three principal landowners were Musgrave on Hartley Fell, Wharton (and from the eighteenth century, Lowther) with interests in Nateby, Wharton and Swaledale and the Clifford interest in Mallerstang and Stainmore.

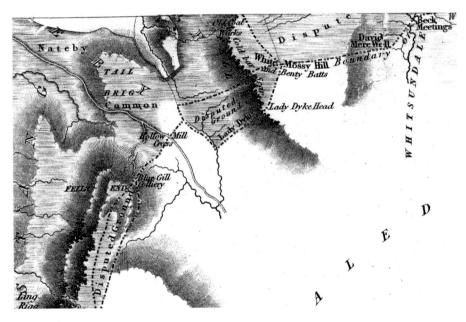

A section of Hodgson's map of Westmorland (1829) indicating the disputed ground on the watershed.

*On the modern 1:25000 OS map a boundary marked as Grey Stone (BS) is located on the Swaledale side
of the watershed. It is marked with "BO 1817" & "FHL1890" and is located below Blue Gill Colliery
on Hodgson's Map. The FHL initials (Frederick Horner Lyell) appear also at the southern end of
Mallerstang at Lady's Pillar - see Chapter 10.*

There is a prominent cairn on the summit of Tailbridge and just south a 'Y' shaped structure
created from limestone most probably for shelter. Other features that are mapped but not so
readily identified on the ground are Lady Dike which seems to be a quite extensive boundary
on the southern perimeter of High Dukerdale and Hollow Mill Cross which lies adjacent to the
B6270.

At the foot of Tailbridge Hill running north from the road are a series of coal excavations marked
as swallow holes on modern maps. There is also a ruinous sheepfold below them. There is then
a wedge of land sloping down west towards Nateby. It is bounded by the B6270 and on its
northern perimeter a large enclosure named Nateby Cow Close which extends into Dukerdale.
This is an early enclosure or vaccary whose original outline has been dated at 1563. It was
further subdivided during the parliamentary enclosure movement of the nineteenth century.
There are a series of gritstone outcrops running laterally across this slope where there are simple
shelters and evidence of coal workings. Great Edge is the most obvious of these outcrops and
this extends over the B6270 where there are more coal workings towards Kitchen Gill.

The first edition 6 inch scale OS map identifies 'cinder kilns' lower down the slope above the road. The Memoir of the Geological Survey for Mallerstang (1891) noted the presence of cinder-ovens and extensive workings for coal used for coke. Some evidence of this burning and the remaining waste can still be found. Lower down and into the limestone there are swallow holes called Blind Gill Holes and adjacent to the road an area called Ore Hill, the site of a quarry and Stephen Grove Mine which is again identified on the 1862 edition of the OS 6 inch map. It is thought to have only been a minor prospect for lead. The word 'grove' has Anglo-Danish origins because miners worked *grooves* or *greaves* and the word carried over to the naming of mines.

Nateby parish belonged to the Whartons (until it was sequestered in 1728) and the fourth Lord (Philip) Wharton did lease some mines in Nateby late in the seventeenth century, the ore (and possibly coke) going to Swaledale for smelting. The first Lord Wharton, Thomas, had purchased the manor of Muker and part of Healaugh from the Crown in 1544 - 6 (during the dissolution of the monasteries) which gave him control of a large portion of upper Swaledale. By the early seventeenth century the estates had passed to his grandson Philip who was instrumental in developing mining in Swaledale and discussed in Chapter 4. In the 1670's the Whartons had moved to dispossess small miners and establish mining on a larger scale and from this time greater investment was made in driving longer levels. It also illustrates the relatively low productivity of the upper Eden mines.

Top: *Looking north into High Dukerdale*

Below: *Old coal excavations on the west flank of Tailbridge Hill above the B6270 Nateby to Keld road.*

Chapter 10

Upper Eden Upland: Mallerstang

Millstone cut out in the Elmgill Crag boulder field

Daniel Defoe passed through Mallerstang early in the eighteenth century and described with horror *this terrible aspect of the hills* when he wrote A Tour through the Whole Island of Great Britain which was published in 1724. His response to the landscape was the same when he reached northern Scotland. In fact Defoe was more interested in material progress than wild hills. He noted approvingly that the town of Kirkby Stephen was involved in a great manufacture of yarn stockings, discussed in Chapter 6. The Romantic appreciation of mountain landscapes was only to develop later at the end of the eighteenth century with William Wordsworth and the *Lake Poets*.

Mallerstang forms a spectacular and continuous skyline of millstone grit with the Eden valley carved out below. The Edge has a series of spectacular scars and corries which merit an outline here. The most northerly scar is Fells End which has been extensively quarried for slate, stone and coal. Below the scar there are extensive tips of debris and also material from moraines thought to have been created during periods of glaciation. In fact moraines are a feature below all the scars. Between Fells End and Bleakham is an area called High Brae where coal has been excavated but it is now an area seldom visited. The next scar to the south is Bleakham, faulted east-west, and a very distinctive feature at this northern end of the Edge. At the base of Lindrigg Scars there is a large moraine. Two principal streams drain down onto Lindrigg from the Edge and merge below the main crags. After heavy rain and with a westerly wind a waterfall below Lindrigg appears like a smoking chimney. Coalwell Scars in contrast to the forbidding overhangs of Lindrigg is divided horizontally by a series of steep grassy levels. Below Coalwell there is a silted lakelet which lies behind another significant moraine. The most extensive faulting on this side of the valley is the area of High Band, High Loven and Hangingstone Scars with fields of boulders and debris on the slopes below particularly under the Loven Scars. Further south there is a massive boulder field, Elmgill Crag, extending further down the lower slopes of the valley. At the end of the Edge is the charmingly named Raven's Nest - a secluded retreat in a rock outcrop - possibly quarried. The naming of areas in upland Mallerstang is not without a bleak realism with descriptions such as *Black Gutter, Foul Gutter* and *The Mires* and also a reminder that even this somewhat intractable landscape has been described with immense care and patience.

The principal geology of upper Eden was briefly outlined in Chapter 8. It has relevance across a much wider area of upland plateau referred to as the Askrigg Block. The generally heavily mineralised rocks of the Askrigg Block form the southern part of the Northern Pennine Orefield which extends from Stainmore in Cumbria to Craven in Yorkshire. The Block consists of an underlying granite mass deep underground which is overlaid by the Yoredale series - a mainly horizontal rock strata laid down in the carboniferous period. The series consist of recurring layers of uplifted sandstone, shales and limestones capped in some cases by millstone grit or gritstone. These layers are also faulted mainly in an east-west configuration which recur moving south from Stainmore to the Bastifell Fault on Hartley Fell, Kitchen Gill between Tailbridge and Fells End at Mallerstang and at Bleakham. The Dent Fault, the most significant fault of the whole area, runs 32 kilometres north-south from Kirkby Stephen to Kirkby Lonsdale and divides the horizontal limestone scars of the Yorkshire Dales from the Howgill Fells formed from the Silurian rocks of the Lake District. The harder rocks of the Dales resisted erosion and remained as isolated remnants in the landscape.

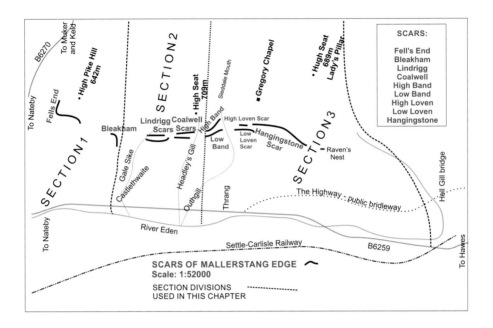

SCARS OF MALLERSTANG EDGE
Scale: 1:52000

SECTION DIVISIONS
USED IN THIS CHAPTER

Looking north to Hangingstone Scar, Mallerstang Edge

The most common examples of resisted erosion are the 3 Peaks of Yorkshire; Ingleborough, Whernside and Pen-Y-Ghent but they are also manifested in the peaks that surround the upper Eden valley particularly Mallerstang Edge and Wild Boar Fell. Older carboniferous limestones also cover this vast area extending down the Eden valley as far as Wharton Hall. Layers of younger limestones and sandstones recur up the fell sides in some cases creating the familiar exposed pavements of Great Scar limestone which characterise much of this landscape. From Wharton the geology changes from limestone to sandstone and can be seen dramatically at Stenkrith Park, Kirkby Stephen, where the river Eden has cut through to red sandstone on the river bed. The local stone here is known as *brockram*, a tough mix of fragments of limestone and sandstone. In terms of mining geology, as already mentioned, the upland is known as the Northern Pennine Orefield extending from Hadrian's Wall down to the limestone around Settle and Pateley Bridge. The Orefield is divided by the Stainmore Pass between Bowes in County Durham and Brough in Cumbria - and its northern portion called the Alston Block.

In the medieval period Mallerstang had the status of forest or, more accurately, *free chase*. Mallerstang Forest was one small component in an extensive network of upland forests across medieval England. More than seventy separate forests have been identified in the uplands during this period. Some responsibility for forest creation lies with the Normans although it seems likely that they had pre-Conquest origins. However, it seems William the Conqueror did establish many forests and a stringent system of rules for their administration under the protection of a separate Forest Law. The whole upland Pennine region contained a network of moorland forest; Stainmore, Swaledale, Wensleydale and Mallerstang in the immediate locality. In the wider area the Lune Forest situated between Tees and Lune and, to the south, the chases of Langstrathdale, Bishopdale, Coverdale and Nidderdale in Yorkshire. In the medieval period forests were expressions of legal status for hunting by feudal overlords who, under royal licence, controlled vast baronial estates. The expression forest referred to their royal control whilst the term *chase* was normally applied to areas under lay or private ownership. In the case of both Mallerstang and Stainmore they belonged to the barony of Westmorland - eventually the Clifford dynasty who came to retain estates in Westmorland and the Craven upland of Yorkshire centred on Skipton Castle. As mentioned the word forest was a legal term rather than a description of woodland or vegetation.

Looking north to Mallerstang Edge from The Highway.

Forests were under royal control and located mainly in lowland England although the Forest of Inglewood was royal forest located to the south of Carlisle in the old county of Cumberland. Inglewood was reputedly of enormous extent and provided for many varieties of game. It began to be reduced in size from 1819 when nearly 30,000 acres were enclosed. However, much upland was *free chase* belonging within the estates of baronial lords. There were also various types of enclosure within these estates. It was usual for the great barons to have a lowland castle with attached or adjacent enclosures or parks and an area for upland hunting. For example, one seat for the barony of Westmorland lay at Appleby Castle and had an enclosed deer park nearby at Flakebridge. At Brougham, another seat for the Westmorland barony, the castle was attached to Whinfell forest and it seems likely that deer began to be contained here as pressure on land intensified after the twelfth century. The upland *chases* for the barony of Westmorland lay more distantly at Stainmore and Mallerstang both with adjacent castles at Brough and Pendragon. Whilst these areas were used for hunting most owners recognised that they also had potential to create income from stock farming or grazing and also, as time progressed, as a frontier for settlement.

In the vicinity of Mallerstang there remain some enclosures created as *vaccaries* for stock farming. Nateby Cow Close, north of the B6270 Nateby to Swaledale road, was originally a cow pasture enclosed from the common before 1590. It was subsequently divided by private agreement in 1857 during the parliamentary enclosure movement. The term *frith* is thought to refer to an earlier type of enclosure used for deer or game in upland forest. *Low Frith* and *High Frith* on the lower flank of Wild Boar Fell were attached to Pendragon Castle. The creation of forest law was a means to distinguish its operation from the common law and to recognise its special status for recreation and hunting. Strictly speaking forest law only held sway in royal forest whilst offences against the privileges of free chase were punishable under common law. Its rights were upheld by foresters. Ridding House, now ruinous, and located north of Great Bell in Mallerstang is said to have been the deer keeper's residence. Nicholls in *The History & Traditions of Mallerstang Forest* notes a fine of £20 imposed on Thomas Knewstubb and others for killing a deer as late as 1665 which suggests that close control was exercised over these areas of lordly privilege. Generally, by the sixteenth century, stock rearing began to take precedence over hunting and there was a gradual retreat of lordly control into the upper reaches of the upland as hill farming settlements began to expand into the valleys. The pressure placed on these areas by cattle and sheep also compromised the ability of deer to survive. Nicholls comments in particular that Swaledale - a chase under the control of the Wharton family - was carefully protected by them and became a last refuge for deer *which remained in considerable numbers northwards from Muker as late as the year 1725*. Ironically the lead smelting mills of Swaledale seem to have contributed to the decline of deer by consuming the woods in the area. By the fifteenth century vaccaries were increasingly leased to tenants and divided into smaller units. By the sixteenth century peasant communities had expanded and hill pasture rights began to be treated as common land or manorial waste. By the early sixteenth century upland dispersed communities such as Mallerstang were well established.

Eleven settlements are listed in rent documents for the manor of Mallerstang at this time. Today the dominant feature of the landscape is the absence of enclosed land except in the valley. Some early examples of enclosure are evident in the vaccaries or cattle enclosures but there are few examples of later enclosure resulting from Act of Parliament. One further type of enclosure is to be found in the upland - the *lonely field*. These are small pockets of enclosed moorland created for hay and grazing. There are examples at Greenlaw near to *The Friths* at Pendragon, in upper Swaledale on Birkdale Common and at Uldale to the south of The Clouds. Many of these remain in use today.

Top: *The lonely field at Greenlaw on the lower slopes of Wild Boar Fell with Mallerstang Edge on the horizon. The barn is now gone but the ground is still in use as pasture.*

Below: *The drawing of The North West view of Pendragon Castle, Samuel & Nathaniel Buck, 1739*

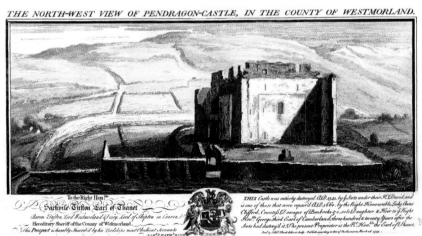

The history of Pendragon is consistent with the contested state of this border region through the centuries. The castle itself is a late Norman pele tower circa 1180 although the first mention of a stone castle seems to be 1314. The site is also associated in myth with the father of King Arthur, Uther Pendragon. The tower was burnt, restored, burnt again but it continued to generate romantic associations. During the Tudor period, interest in Arthurianism was strong. George Clifford, third earl of Cumberland was appointed Queens Champion in 1590 by Elizabeth I. The handover was made in the tiltyard at Whitehall Palace and earl George appeared in white as the Knight of Pendragon Castle accompanied by the magician Merlin and, perhaps, Uther Pendragon. George remained Queens Champion until her death in 1603 and used the Pendragon identity more than once. Pendragon lay ruined for over one hundred years before being repaired for habitation by Lady Anne Clifford in 1660. She also built the neighbouring bridge over the Eden, an enclosing wall around the castle and closer to the river were stables, coach and brew-houses, now only mounds. Ironically Lady Anne, who was born in 1590, had been excluded from most of the Clifford estates when her father, earl George, died. The estate passed to his brother Francis and a long legal battle was fought for her to finally gain control following Francis' death. After her death the castle was stripped of its lead by the earl of Thanet in 1687 to reduce the cost of upkeep. For nearly three hundred years the ruin deteriorated until it was privately purchased in 1963 from when what remained was consolidated and preserved. Pendragon was originally three storeys above a ground floor basement. The castle is scheduled as a Grade1 Ancient Monument.

The first, northern, section of Mallerstang consists of the lower hills bordering the B6259 known as Great Bell and Bells which occupy the lower ground west of Mallerstang Edge. To the east of Great Bell gently rising ground culminates in Fells End and the plateau of Mallerstang Edge, High Pike Hill and Bleakham.

The main feature of the area of Great Bell and Bells are the old lead workings both on the lower flanks just east of Dalefoot and around the summit of Great Bell itself. In *Lakes & Cumbria Mines Guide* Tyler identifies two sets of workings. The older are on, and around, Great Bell. These extend above and below the line of the exposed limestone of Long Crag. There has been extensive hushing behind Long Crag and a perpendicular cross cut has been made across it as a test.

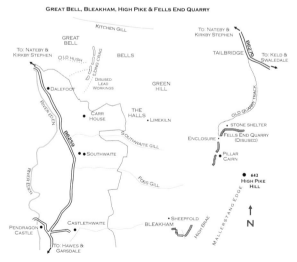

Great Bell and Long Crag with extensive hushing.

There are different accounts of the viability of the mining here perhaps explained by the fact that the earliest workings were primitive but still worth small scale exploitation. In *Mallerstang: A Westmorland Dale* (1965) Mary M Thompson describes Southwaite as the oldest site for a farmouse in the dale with a continuous history dating back to 1346 in the reign of Edward III. Thompson notes that when the lead mines were worked on the Bells there were five dwelling houses on the site with one house inhabited by two separate families. In a brief section on *Mines* she suggests that a very poor lead was worked for many years by the Pease Company of Darlington. This seems to corroborate an earlier account by the Rev. Nicholls in *The History & Traditions of Mallerstang Forest* (1883) who suggests that after initial failures the Pease' offered a reward for finding a vein of lead and one Jno. Scott of Southwaite found one such pocket which was worked successfully. It is not clear when this was but the Pease company were operating in the area in connection with the Stainmore Railway. Tyler dates the older workings as possibly pre-1750 and the later ones, referred to as Dalefoot workings, at around 1860-80. These later workings are certainly not recorded on the first edition OS six inch map of 1862 whereas the second edition does show a track that zig-zags up to them from the roadside above Dalefoot (previously Dalefoot was called Bluegrass).

Pendragon Castle today

The location of Fells End slate quarry is spectacular with a commanding position over the Eden valley and Tailbridge. It is situated on a ridge at about 550 metres and below the northerly summit of High Pike. Originally there was an access track to it from Tailbridge Neck. Most of this track remains on the ground. It crosses Kitchen Gill and becomes indistinct in boggy ground before continuing to traverse the base of Fells End crags and then zig-zags up the hillside finally doubling back on itself above the same crags.

The quarry is extensive but there are few records. There is significant debris below the quarry, ruined shelters and a large walled enclosure possibly used for pack ponies or sheep. One, now roofless, shelter has a chimney flue. There is a distinctive narrow cylinder-shaped cairn further south on the edge of the hillside and nearby what appears to be the remains of a small reservoir or dam. Scattered over the area are slates and flags. There is also a more unusual shelter below the northern edge of Fells End which is very well camouflaged and is only visible from above. It is situated just above the old quarry track as it traverses across the base of Fells End crags. The shelter consists of a small single chamber and a smaller adjoining unit. It looks as if it would have been roofed with flags. It is quite unlike other structures in the area and is also well concealed.

Top: *Stone shelter on slightly lower ground just north of Fells End Quarry. Tailbridge Hill and Nateby Common form the middle distance.*

Below: *Ruined buildings at Fells End Quarry. A large stone enclosure is just out of shot to the right and the distant pillar cairn stands part way to Bleakham Scar.*

A number of old coal workings occur in this section. There are old shafts between the B6270 and Kitchen Gill. The Kitchen Gill seam is thought to be 12 - 15 inches thick. This seam and others higher up towards Mallerstang Edge were noted in the Geological Survey Memoirs for Mallerstang (1891). It referred to a Fells End coal seam to be more or less continuous to the colliery at Outhgill. The survey also noted coal at a location on the Yorkshire side of Fells End at Blue Gill. It would seem that this may also have been worked; a Blue Gill colliery is marked on Hodgson's map of Westmorland (1828) a section of which is reproduced in Chapter 9. Whilst there are few records there is some evidence of surface coal working between Fells End and Bleakham in the area called High Brae at about 600 metres. There is conspicuous spoil in two sections above the site of the abandoned stone trough (see photograph Chapter 8) and the faint remains of a track that may have serviced this remote location.

The second section of the Mallerstang Scars is more or less bounded by Gale Sike to the north and Headley's Gill to the south. The principal features on open fell consist of the summit of High Seat on Mallerstang Edge, the Lindrigg and Coalwell Scars and the scars of High Band and Low Band.

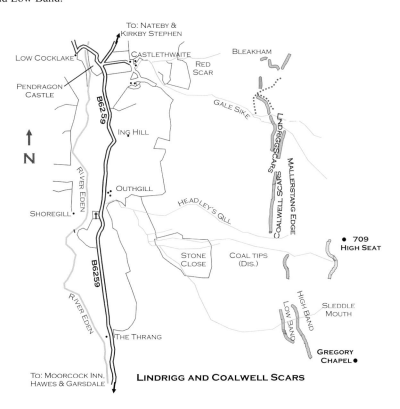

LINDRIGG AND COALWELL SCARS

Stone Close on Mallerstang Common - Headley's Gill and Sloe Brae Gill traverse the northern edge of the enclosure.

Mallerstang Colliery was located on the fellside below Trough Riggs (between Coalwell Scars and High Band) just east of Outhgill. There is an old track to it from the village which crosses Headley's Gill and winds uphill adjacent to Stone Close.

Apart from the surface spoil heaps there are few remains of the colliery now which was situated just south of Sloe Brae Gill. There were floods in both 2005 and 2007 which brought considerable debris onto the site. The lower entrance shaft with a stone arch was just visible at the time of writing but the large stone house in front of it has almost disappeared. The Geological Survey of Mallerstang (1891) noted that there was a continuous seam of coal from Fells End to Outhgill. The pit was opened in the 1820's. There are some records of the management of Outhgill Colliery by the Horne brothers in the period 1859-63 and an agreement signed by them with Sir Richard Tufton of Appleby Castle (successors to the Clifford estates). The agreement extended a lease in consideration of the cost of opening out the mine but the project took a downturn and was abandoned leaving debts. It is possible that one or two of the Horne brothers eventually left for Australia.

At Sleddale Mouth (named Steddale Mouth on more recent OS maps) is the location for the discovery of a cache of Roman coins, known as the Mallerstang Hoard, in September 1926. (See Chapter 1). The precise location for this find is unknown.

Above: A bield on the fellside below Lindrigg Scars identified as a form of shelter or refuge. Wild Boar Fell forms the horizon for the picture left.

Below: The ruins of Mallerstang Colliery after flooding in recent years. The stone arched entrance is to the lower level and the substantial stone building has all but disappeared.

The third section of the Mallerstang Scars covers Hugh Seat, High and Low Loven Scar, Hangingstone Scar and Ravens Nest.

This southern section of Mallerstang is to a great extent the wildest and, below the scars, the least visited. But the track from Aisgill to Hell Gill is excellent for access to Mallerstang Edge from the south and The High Way is also a good access route as it traverses the lower slopes of the valley from The Thrang. Looking east from the road the prospect is a series of faulted scars and heavily boulder-strewn ground. The curiously named Elmgill Crag describes a massive boulder field below Hangingstone Scar. There seems little evidence of human activity here although there are two (undocumented) sheepfolds hidden away on Elmgill and at least one rudimentary shelter in the corrie below High Loven Scar. Discarded millstones have been found in the Elmgill boulder field. The area is rich in historical associations. The valley was an important droving route and further south, in Yorkshire, The High Way becomes a spectacular high level road with ruined drover's inns such as High Dyke. The Clifford dynasty had a lasting impact on Mallerstang and Pendragon Castle was restored more than once following raids by the Scots. Its last restoration was initiated by Lady Anne Clifford in 1660 and she was also responsible for Lady's Pillar on Hugh Seat *a structure of unknown form built of squared stone.* It had fallen at some point but one of the stones bears her married initials A.P. (Anne Pembroke) and the date 1664. Another stone bears the mark "FHL 1890" and according to Ella Pontefract's Swaledale are the initials of Frederick Horner Lyell a Lord of the Manor on the Yorkshire side.

Lady's Pillar

In the 1950's correspondence in the local press initiated by F.W. Parrott of Kirkby Stephen reiterated a plea for this relic to be preserved. It was used as a mark for the Westmorland-Yorkshire boundary and defined the limit of Lady Anne Clifford's Mallerstang estate. The pillar lies close to the summit of Hugh Seat named after Hugh de Morville the first recorded Norman Lord of Mallerstang. Hugh de Morville was one of the four knights who murdered Archbishop Thomas a Beckett in Canterbury Cathedral in 1170.

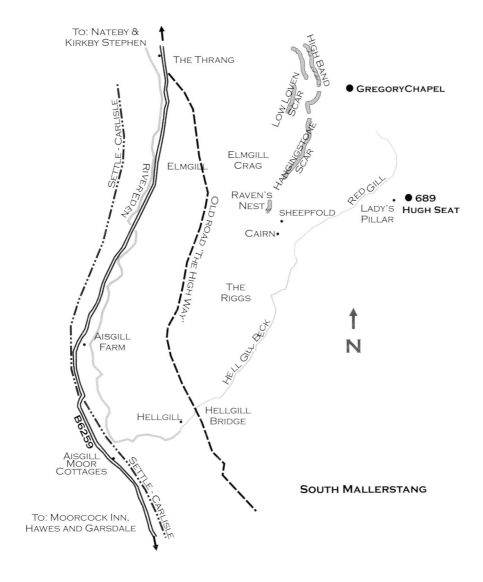

TO: NATEBY &
KIRKBY STEPHEN

THE THRANG

HIGH BAND

LOW LOVEN SCAR

● GREGORY CHAPEL

SETTLE - CARLISLE

RIVER EDEN

OLD ROAD 'THE HIGH WAY'

ELMGILL

ELMGILL CRAG

HANGINGSTONE SCAR

RAVEN'S NEST

SHEEPFOLD

RED GILL

LADY'S PILLAR

● 689
HUGH SEAT

CAIRN

THE RIGGS

HELL GILL BECK

N

AISGILL FARM

B6259

HELLGILL

HELLGILL BRIDGE

AISGILL MOOR COTTAGES

SETTLE - CARLISLE

SOUTH MALLERSTANG

TO: MOORCOCK INN,
HAWES AND GARSDALE

Raven's Nest, Mallerstang

Chapter 11

Upper Eden Upland: Wild Boar Fell & The Clouds

Cairns on Yoadcomb Scar, Wild Boar Fell. The Yorkshire peaks of Whernside and Ingleborough form the far horizon.

Unlike the other summits dealt with in the two previous chapters, on Hartley Fell and Mallerstang, Wild Boar Fell stands in contrast as Eden's finest mountain. It is a remarkable landmark and its outline is both visible and easily recognised from all directions being set in an extensive and spacious landscape. The views from the summit are superb; in settled weather the silhouettes of the Three Peaks of Yorkshire lie to the southeast, to the west the northern Howgills and the central fells of the Lake District, to the east fine views across to Mallerstang Edge and, ranging north, the north western flank of the Pennine range capped by its highest peak Cross Fell. Approaching Mallerstang from Nateby, Wild Boar Fell looks like a mountain particularly in snow. The rocky precipices of White Walls culminating in The Nab and its ancient cairn. The summit proper is set on the west side of a large plateau and is more readily observed in outline to the west from Ash Fell where the vast apron of the mountain's west flank towers over Greenrigg and Ravenstonedale Common. Travelling north to Aisgill on the B6259 there is another breathtaking panorama of Aisgill Head, The Band and High White Scar.

In terms of geology there is a continuity of the same rock series as occurs across the valley on Mallerstang Edge. The Mallerstang Memoir of the Geological Survey (1891) noted that the grits and shales on Mallerstang Edge (High Band, High Loven Scar and Hangingstone Scar) are equivalent to the strata on the precipices on the eastern edge of Wild Boar Fell at The Nab, High White Scar and The Band. It may not seem obvious but the highest point on the upper Eden fells is at High Seat on Mallerstang whose summit consists of sandstone with a thin layer of limestone at its base. The plateau of Wild Boar summit, on the other hand, is grit and extends for about a mile from north-east to south-west. Amongst the grit strata occur various shales and coal seams and even in this inhospitable environment there are the remains of workings for coal and minerals such as copper. This replicates the experience on the other side of Mallerstang where coal seams have been worked at Fells End and on Hartley Fell. There is a coal seam high on Wild Boar Fell and a pit is marked on the modern OS map north east of Sand Tarn (even though difficult to locate). There are also shallow quarries on the summit plateau not far from the trig point. A partially finished millstone is located above Sand Tarn. On the eastern flank of Wild Boar below High Dolphinsty there is an enclosure named Lordburn Close which has been identified as a site for lead or copper and there are the ruins of a (mine) house. The first edition 6 inch scale map identifies a hush below the enclosure. But how productive this trial was is unclear. It probably dates to the eighteenth century. Earlier maps identify Colliers Gutter to the west of Little Fell where there were also coal shafts in 1641 according to past enquiries. It would seem, however, that more productive seams were worked in the locality on Baugh Fell and at Tan Hill.

Millstone cut out above Sand Tarn, Wild Boar Fell.

Sand Tarn is located at 640 metres (2100 feet), north west of Wild Boar Fell summit at 708 metres (2322 feet).

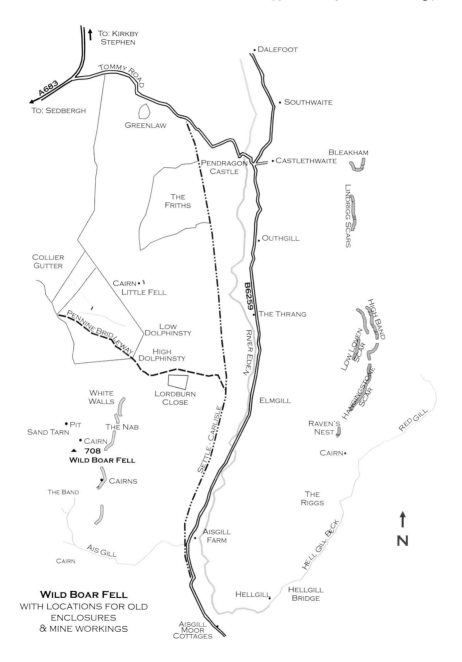

TO: KIRKBY STEPHEN

TOMMY ROAD

A683

TO: SEDBERGH

GREENLAW

DALEFOOT

SOUTHWAITE

BLEAKHAM

PENDRAGON CASTLE

CASTLETHWAITE

THE FRITHS

OUTHGILL

LINDRIGG SCARS

COLLIER GUTTER

CAIRN • LITTLE FELL

PENNINE BRIDLEWAY

LOW DOLPHINSTY

HIGH DOLPHINSTY

B6259

THE THRANG

RIVER EDEN

HIGH BAND

LOW LOVEN SCAR

HANGINGSTONE SCAR

WHITE WALLS

LORDBURN CLOSE

ELMGILL

RED GILL

PIT

SAND TARN

THE NAB

RAVEN'S NEST

SETTLE - CARLISLE

CAIRN •

CAIRN •

▲ 708

WILD BOAR FELL

CAIRNS

THE BAND

THE RIGGS

AIS GILL

HELL GILL BECK

CAIRN

AISGILL FARM

N

WILD BOAR FELL

WITH LOCATIONS FOR OLD
ENCLOSURES
& MINE WORKINGS

HELLGILL

HELLGILL BRIDGE

AISGILL MOOR COTTAGES

Looking south to Wild Boar Fell from Little Fell. The enclosure wall at High Dolphinsty is in the middle distance.

There are two outliers on the Wild Boar Fell ridge both forming the base of millstone grit. To the south lies Swarth Fell (681m) and Little Fell (559m) to the north. On the descent north Little Fell is preceded by two east-west faults at High and Low Dolphinsty now connected by the outer edge of an enclosure wall.

Centuries ago Wild Boar Fell formed part of Mallerstang Forest described in Chapter 10. Mallerstang Common covers the upland on both sides of the river Eden and would have formed part of the area of lordly retreat originally reserved for hunting. Indeed the name Wild Boar Fell is believed to originate from when the last of that species met its end at the hand of Sir Richard Musgrave. A tusk found in an excavated tomb at St Stephen's in Kirkby Stephen is said to have been where he was buried along with his trophy. It is through the noble families of the district that a good deal of its history is woven. The principal families of North Westmorland all held manorial courts in Kirkby Stephen by the eighteenth century although the history of their emergence occurred over centuries. Kirkby Stephen was divided between three lordships; the earls of Lonsdale (Lowther), the earls of Thanet (previously the Clifford dynasty) and the Musgrave family. Manorial courts administered these communities through patronage and obligation. A complex network of lineage and kin relationships regulated economic, social and political affairs. The values that sustained this way of life were grounded in maintaining status and hierarchy. In *The Family, Sex and Marriage in England 1500 - 1800* (1977) Lawrence Stone singled out the weakly governed upland areas of the north of England as the location for a culture based on lineage and lordship in the sixteenth century. Where the state and the law were weak this alternative support system flourished. The great and noble northern 'houses' of Neville, Clifford, Percy and Dacre held a central role although their influence was soon to go into decline as political power became more centralised. Over the long term the political history of the uplands is in part a story of the displacement of noble privilege and the creation of communities that slowly gained greater control over the use of the upland for farming and settlement mainly in scattered townships. As we have seen Cumbria in particular was historically marginal and only became English in the twelfth century after it was taken from Scotland and even in the fourteenth century it was still subject to border raiding.

The barony of Westmorland, later Appleby, was originally held for the Crown by Hugh de Morvill (hence Hugh's Seat on Mallerstang) on behalf of Henry II but he was ejected in 1174. There were further changes of control between the Crown and other holders until 1203 when Robert de Veteripont gained Appleby, Brough and the Bailiwick of Westmarieland. Later, under King John, it seems there was an introduction of military service to the barony. The Veteripont lordship passed down to a grand-daughter who married Roger de Clifford in 1269. Confusingly the Clifford dynasty acquired the title of earls of Cumberland in spite of their attachment to Westmorland. The title passed down through the Clifford family and, following a long legal battle, to Lady Anne Clifford. The estate had been financially compromised by her father, George Clifford, thirteenth lord and third earl of Cumberland (1558-1605) who had incurred debt to fund his maritime interests and privateering ventures which were privately financed although they were effectively officially sanctioned anti-Spanish ventures.

Although he was never a major political figure, George was a loyal servant to his queen. In 1590 Elizabeth appointed him as Queen's Champion and he styled himself as the Knight of Pendragon Castle. His daughter, Lady Anne, was an only child (two sons had died young) and at George Clifford's death his estate passed to his brother Francis Clifford to continue the male line and preserve the inheritance. This outcome was vigorously challenged by his daughter. Eventually the estate passed to her at Francis'death and she became responsible for a belated restoration of this northern estate and its properties. Anne's daughter Margaret married John Tufton, Earl of Thanet, in 1629.

Two other and lesser families that originally served in an official capacity, and lived close to Kirkby Stephen, were Musgrave and Wharton. Both have chapels in Kirkby Stephen parish church. The Musgrave chapel is fifteenth century whilst the Wharton chapel is sixteenth. Both families originally served within the dynastic northern network of Clifford, Dacre and Percy. In both cases they gained advancement under Henry VIII's policy of promoting 'new men' to counterbalance the power, rivalry and feuding of the northern barons. Sir Thomas Musgrave had been imprisoned in Carlisle Castle for a forest offence in 1334 but following this misdemeanour he developed a career in official employment and was active in Anglo-Scots border hostilities. In 1353 he fortified Hartley Castle which had frequently been attacked by the Scots. Sir Richard Musgrave turned the castle into a mansion but by 1677 the family had moved to Eden Hall and Hartley Castle fell into ruin. As has been noted previously the Wharton family also prospered under Henry VIII and Sir Thomas Wharton succeeded to the post of Warden of the West March when Border administration was reorganised in 1537. With this appointment both Clifford and Musgrave were passed over and the Wharton family acquired considerable estates in Cumberland, Westmorland and Yorkshire. The Wharton estates were confiscated when the last Duke of Wharton was accused of high treason by supporting the restoration of the Stuarts. The Wharton estates in Cumbria including parts of Kirkby Stephen, Wharton and Ravenstonedale were sold to Robert Lowther in 1728.

The reasons why the upper Eden upland can be said to have a distinct identity have been covered in various ways in previous chapters. Not least has been the historic remoteness and isolation of this upland area, the network of kin and lineage relationships which dominated its socio- economic arrangements (in the absence of more centralised control) and the system of land tenure known as customary right. It is tempting to suggest that the landscape also contributed. The landscape is spacious and largely unenclosed. The cultivation of the upland, although privately owned, was worked in common. The isolated rural communities that grew in the valleys managed an agriculture on ground that was intractable and only suitable for hill grazing. The area had been host to temporary occupation from pre-historic times although in the first 500 years of the first millennium it was probably either unused or under-utilised.

Between Wild Boar Fell and the more southerly Baugh Fell lies Uldale, (wolf-dale) which is adjacent to Grisedale, a remote branch of Garsdale near Sedbergh. Its name suggests an earlier period when wolves occupied and hunted this territory. The precise extent of a Roman presence remains unclear but a Scandinavian influx in the eighth and ninth centuries left a more permanent mark with regard to settlement and in place- names. In Mallerstang the first manorial documents date from 1315 and refer to dwellings at Southwaite. Earlier these upland valleys would have supported summer grazing possibly under monastic control on lease from baronial lords who used these retreats for hunting. Slowly these upland areas were colonised as it became necessary to tenant them on fixed rents. The system of land tenure that developed, customary tenant right, provided a measure of independence and security for tenants although landowners remained powerful and dominant as they emerged from the medieval period. Customary right would eventually place some restriction on a landowner's ability to introduce changes in the agriculture of the region. The Cistercian monks in particular favoured the hard work involved in cultivating marginal land and are known to have been granted leases in Grisedale. Three communities lie in the immediate shadow of Wild Boar Fell; Grisedale, Mallerstang and Ravenstonedale. Mallerstang has already been discussed in the previous chapter. Grisedale is an even more isolated upland valley on the northern edge of upper Wensleydale. The passing of the farming community here has been acknowledged in Barry Cockcroft's *The Dale that Died* (1975). A later account is provided in *The Silent Stream* by John Banks (1991). Grisedale remains just outside the scope of this guide but its brief inclusion here is merited by its remarkable history and the austerity of its landscape. What is left of the sixteen farms once occupied can be traversed on public footpaths and many are now ruined. There is a Quaker burial ground near the head of the valley between West Scale and East Scale farms (Skali a Norse word meaning temporary shelter). The farm buildings here have been restored. Further down the valley at Moor Rigg and adjacent to Grisedale Beck is the site of a former Quaker Meeting House which was built in 1706 and closed in 1870 when it transferred to Garsdale. About 1886 a flood reduced the building to a pile of rubble which Methodists used to build a new chapel closer to the road. It bears the date 1889. The community that flourished here began to struggle towards the end of the nineteenth century and decline continued after 1945.

At Ravenstonedale a pile of stones at Fell End (NY735009) mark the remains of another Quaker Meeting House built in 1705. A stable and loft were added later in 1710. A burial ground is next to the site under a line of trees. There was another Quaker burial ground at Dovengill on the side road about one mile to the south. The Fell End Meeting House was closed in 1793 and demolished in 1899. The Meeting had moved to a hamlet called Narthwaite a few miles down the valley where a room above a barn was used and continued until 1907. In terms of history each of these communities thus shared a religious identity rooted in the emergence of conflicts over non-conformity in the seventeenth century and struggles associated with land tenure and agrarian poverty. Geographical and political isolation and the effects of the colonisation of marginal land provided the basis for a shared culture from earlier times. But each community was different. Ravenstonedale manor had originally been endowed to Gilbertine monks and at the dissolution was acquired by the Whartons of Wharton Hall.

Its point of reference was Kirkby Stephen and the Eden valley as was Mallerstang, a Clifford manor. Grisedale changed from a monastic to a Crown manor and was eventually let to Lord Scrope of Bolton in Yorkshire. The Dissolution of the Monasteries created major economic changes and a reaction amongst the inhabitants of these dales. The Pilgrimage of Grace in 1536/7 had been an attempt to address these changes and was ruthlessly suppressed by Sir Thomas (later Lord) Wharton and Henry VIII and is described in Chapter 3.

Pressure on land continued. John Breay in *Light in the Dales* notes that by 1315 the foundations for cattle farming were laid in Mallerstang. By the early sixteenth century there were eleven customary farms in the valley. Demesne land of the manor, held by the baronial Cliffords of Appleby Castle, included the castle garth at Pendragon and The Friths on the lower flank of Wild Boar Fell. By 1597 these eleven farms had been divided into fifty four tenancies. By 1604 the earl of Cumberland, the Clifford overlord of Mallerstang parish, was in debt as a result of his privateering ventures and all his estates, including Craven in Yorkshire, were under scrutiny to review rentals. A similar process of extracting value from tenants had been exercised by Philip Wharton in the adjacent manors of Grisedale, Ravenstonedale and Wharton. Bad harvests, plague and poverty had also taken its toll in these districts and the period of the Civil War created further uncertainty. A moderate movement of religious dissent was led by Philip Lord Wharton and his Presbyterian faction which had already seen the establishment of protestant Grammar Schools in Kirkby Stephen and Sedbergh. But a more radical movement developed which drew on the existing discontent of the upper Eden valley and was led by the Quaker, George Fox who visited the area and created meetings in Ravenstonedale and

Grisedale in 1652. Many individuals travelled these dales to worship and it is known that there were Quaker households in Mallerstang who attended in Ravenstonedale. It is thought that a meeting may have been held at Outhgill or Shoregill.

Why dissent arose in these remote dales is a question posed by historians given the often greater pressures to conform but when the history and geography of this area are considered it perhaps becomes easier to appreciate how its particular identity has been sustained.

Ravenstonedale Clouds are the westernmost point of the Askrigg Block containing lead and copper bearing veins. The mineral workings are split into different areas and seem to have differing histories. From north to south The Clouds are known as Stennerskeugh Clouds, Clouds and Fell End Clouds. The whole is a complex of limestone scars and pavements located adjacent to the Dent Fault between Wild Boar Fell and The Howgills. Naturally exposed limestone, ancient field boundaries and mine workings create a spectacular combination of wildness and cultivation set against the western flank of Wild Boar Fell. Enclosures, remains of earlier subdivisions and old tracks all contribute to an impression that the landscape has been

CLOUDS, RAVENSTONEDALE
WITH APPROXIMATE LOCATIONS OF OLD
LEAD WORKINGS

Clouds, Ravenstonedale, Cumbria

Looking north to Fell End Clouds. Hushing has eroded the exposed limestone. The dots on the skyline are fell ponies.

A solitary tree grows in the exposed limestone.

Looking north from Dale Slack.

An old enclosure with fell ponies. It is identified on the first edition six inch map just south west of Dale Slack.

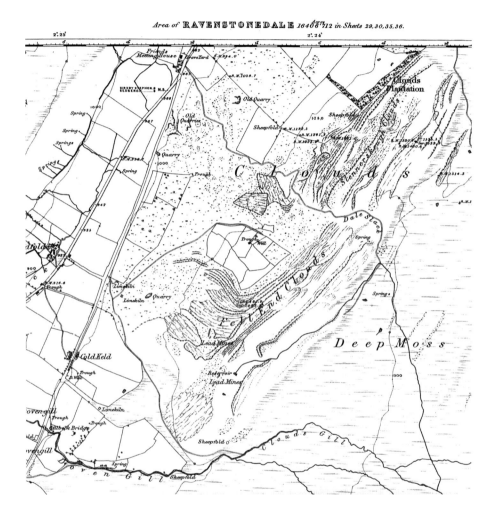

Detail of Clouds, Ravenstonedale from the first edition six inch to one mile Ordnance Survey sheet XXXVI, East Ward (1861). Note the detail for identifying old lead mining sites at Fell End Clouds. The remains of the reservoir and leat feeding into it are still visible on the ground. Also note on the A683 at the top of the map Friends Meeting House (Quaker) which is now demolished. The adjacent burial ground remains as a separate plot filled with mature trees.

Not to scale.

Cumbria Archive Centre, Kendal

exploited over hundreds of years if not millennia. The Street is a name associated with Roman routes and in this case it linked Lancaster and Brough. It suggests an inherited Romano-British landscape. Whilst the term *Clouds* might lead us to imagine that it names the overall shape of the landscape this term has also been associated with mining activity as far back as the first millennium if not the Roman period. The *Clouds* place name is known to occur in various places in the Pennines which are associated with mining or iron-ore extraction. For example Yvonne Luke has identified in Yorkshire; *Arncliffe* and *Hawkswick Clowder* in Littondale, Grassington. *Rear Clouts* near Appletreewick and *Shining Cloud, Five Clouds* and *Hen Clouds* in Derbyshire. (*Forgotten Clouds and Mining Landscapes of the First Millennium AD*, 'British Mining Memoirs (78), 2005.) Overall, however, the history of mining in the Ravenstonedale area is not well documented and accurate datings are difficult.

Ravenstonedale Clouds has been the most productive source for minerals (mainly lead) on the west side of the Eden valley although trials elsewhere have been attempted. Even so it appears the yields were never very productive. The most extensive lead workings occur on the Fell End Clouds scrins (mineral deposits in vertical or steeply dipping fractures) at the southern end of the ridge where miniature gorges have been excavated. Just to the north are the faint remains of a reservoir (marked on the first edition 6 inch OS sheet) and a conduit which runs a long way back along the back of the ridge. It is possible that some of these workings are the earliest. Some of this area, referred to in the British Geological Survey (Northern Pennine Orefield Vol 2, 1985) is thought to have been worked before the seventeenth century and the remains of a bole hill (small scale lead smelting bonfires) were found but it was thought that the lack of output excluded anything more than surface working. The Survey noted four main veins; for lead - Fell End Clouds scrins, Johnson's vein, Clouds vein and copper in Clouds North vein. There was thought to be a small output of copper. There are other workings in the vicinity of Dale Slack (a small valley bisecting the ridge and more intensive 'modern' mining at the northern end. Some of the working has been documented (by N G Robinson) and again confirms that open cast trenches were most commonly used in earlier trials. (N.G. Robinson, 'Ravenstonedale' in British Mining Memoirs (41), 1990.)

The London Lead Company acquired a lease from Lord Lonsdale in 1802 but the results were disappointing. Further efforts were made in 1806 and in 1870 Henry Pease of Darlington took a lease but this was given up in 1875. A last attempt was made in 1884 when a copper vein was discovered which was later found to be unpromising.

Further Reading

There is an extensive literature available for anyone interested in the subjects discussed in these essays. However, it is probably useful to point out that much of it is dispersed within more comprehensive works dealing with Cumbria or the Lake District or other parts of the country on subjects like the Pilgrimage of Grace. There is also a wealth of information in antiquarian and historical journals but these can sometimes be difficult to access.

A starting point with the latter would be the The Cumberland & Westmorland Antiquarian & Archaeological Society whose annual Transactions (CW1, 2 & 3) now span three centuries. The Old Series Vol. I to XVI (1866 - 1900) for which there is an Index, the New Series 1901 - 2000 (with an Index for 1960 - 1989) and the Third Series from 2001 - the present. There are also useful articles in academic journals such as Northern History and Economic History Review.

J. Nicholson and R. Burn's The History and Antiquities of Cumberland and Westmorland Volume 1 originally published in 1777 is useful and was reprinted in 1976. Also of value is Later Records of North Westmorland by John F Curwen (Kendal, 1932).

A useful original survey for archaeology is An Inventory of the Historical Monuments in Westmorland published by The Royal Commission on Historical Monuments (1936). More recent detailed surveys include Stainmore: The Archaeology of a North Pennine Pass by Blaise Vyner (pub. Tees Archaeology & English Heritage (2001) and The Archaeology of North West England by Mark Brennand ed. (2006). General surveys for Cumbria include The Lake Counties 1500 - 1830: A Social & Economic History by C.M.L. Bouch and G.P. Jones (Manchester, 1961) and Prelates and People of the Lake Counties: A History of the Diocese of Carlisle 1133 - 1933 by C.M.L. Bouch (Kendal, 1948).

For the Border there are important journal articles in Northern History 'The Anglo- Scottish Border' by G.W.S. Barrow (1966, 21 - 43) and 'The pacification of the English borders, 1593 - 1628' (1977, 59 - 160). A useful older work is The lord wardens of the Marches of England and Scotland by H.Pease (London, 1913). A more popular work is G.M. Fraser, The steel bonnets: The story of the Anglo-Scottish border reivers (London, 1995).

The original two volume and definitive work on the Pilgrimage of Grace published in 1915 is by M.H. & R. Dodds, with the same title. Two more recent accounts by academic historians are R.W. Hoyle, The Pilgrimage of Grace and the Politics of the 1530's, (Oxford, 2001) and Michael Bush, The Pilgrimage of Grace: A study of the rebel armies of 1536 (Manchester, 1996). A more popular work by G. Moorhouse is The Pilgrimage of Grace: the rebellion that shook Henry VIII's throne (London, 2003).

An important article about the first Lord Wharton by M.E. James is Change and continuity in the Tudor north: The rise of Thomas first Lord Wharton, Borthwick Paper 27 (York, 1965) and J.J. Scarisbrick's Henry VIII (London, 1968) provides valuable background for the context of Wharton's career.

Two useful articles about Wharton's deer parks are M. Blackett-Ord, 'Lord Wharton's deer park walls', CW2, 1986, 133 - 9 and R.W. Hoyle, 'Thomas first Lord Wharton's parks at Ravenstonedale and Wharton, CW2, 1995, 111 -118.

Chapter Six ' Kirkby Stephen' is the only referenced chapter and contains a comprehensive list of the main books and articles consulted in its preparation. The chapter that follows 'The Fawcett Sketchbook' acknowledges the debt to a preceding work entitled Kirkby Stephen by Anne & Alec Swailes (1985).

For the final chapters about the landscape of the Upper Eden upland a number of more local works were useful and these are mentioned below. In addition the work of the University of Lancaster landscape historians is acknowledged. Examples include A.J.L. Winchester, 'Moorland forests of medieval England' in I.D. Whyte and A.J.L. Winchester (eds.), Society, Landscape and Environment in upland Britain (Society for Landscape Studies, 2004) and work by Ian Whyte including Transforming Fell and Valley: Landscape and Parliamentary Enclosure in North West England (Lancaster, 2003).

Works more particular to Kirkby Stephen and the Upper Eden valley include antiquarian accounts by the Rev. W. Nicholls, The History and Traditions of Ravenstonedale (1877) and The History and Traditions of Mallerstang Forest and Pendragon Castle (1883). Mallerstang: A Westmorland Dale by Mary M. Thompson was published in 1965 and updates the account provided by Nicholls. Also of interest is Historical Kirkby Stephen and North Westmorland by R.R. Sowerby (1950), Mallerstang Dale by John Hamilton (1993) and A History of Kirkby Stephen by Douglas Birkbeck (2000). From Hellgill to Bridgend: Aspects of economic and social change in the Upper Eden Valley, 1840 - 95 by Margaret E. Shepherd (2003) is more recent and very comprehensive. Stephen Walker's Nine Standards: Ancient Cairns or Modern Folly (2008) is an attempt to reach a conclusion about this local landmark. Finally, an important and probably neglected work which was published in haste prior to the author's death is Light in the Dales: Studies in religious dissent and land tenure (Vols. 2 & 3) by John Breay (1996).

For mining in the area a useful brief survey is contained in The Lakes and Cumbria Mines Guide by Ian Tyler (2006) and in the later Cross Fell and the Mines of the Cumbrian Pennines (2013). A more detailed survey is in British Mining No. 91: Mines of the West Pennines by Richard and Sam Murphy (Northern Mine Research Society, 2011). A superbly documented account of the legal dispute between Thomas, first Marquess of Wharton and Reginald Marriott over mining rights at Grinton, Swaledale is in 'The Great Trial': ASwaledale Lead Mining dispute in the Court of Exchequer, 1705 - 1708 by Tim Gates ed. (Yorkshire Archaeological Society/Boydell Press, 2012).